Basics of Logic

BASICS OF LOGIC

First Edition

ARACELI NEUNER, PH.D.
San Diego State University

SAN DIEGO

Bassim Hamadeh, CEO and Publisher
Mieka Portier, Senior Acquisitions Editor
Michelle Piehl, Senior Project Editor
Susana Christie, Senior Developmental Editor
Jeanine Rees, Production Editor
Emely Villavicencio, Senior Graphic Designer
XYZ, Licensing Coordinator
Stephanie Adams, Senior Marketing Program Manager
Natalie Piccotti, Director of Marketing
Kassie Graves, Senior Vice President, Editorial
Jamie Giganti, Director of Academic Publishing

Copyright © 2024 by Cognella, Inc. All rights reserved. No part of this publication may be reprinted, reproduced, transmitted, or utilized in any form or by any electronic, mechanical, or other means, now known or hereafter invented, including photocopying, microfilming, and recording, or in any information retrieval system without the written permission of Cognella, Inc. For inquiries regarding permissions, translations, foreign rights, audio rights, and any other forms of reproduction, please contact the Cognella Licensing Department at rights@cognella.com.

Trademark Notice: Product or corporate names may be trademarks or registered trademarks and are used only for identification and explanation without intent to infringe.

Cover image copyright © 2020 iStockphoto LP/m.elyoussoufi.

Printed in the United States of America.

Brief Contents

CHAPTER 1	Logic and the Components of Arguments	1
CHAPTER 2	Deduction, Validity, and Soundness	11
CHAPTER 3	Categorical Reasoning	20
CHAPTER 4	The Square of Opposition	32
CHAPTER 5	Translation into Standard-Form Categorical	41
CHAPTER 6	Three-Circle Venn Diagrams	51
CHAPTER 7	Propositional Logic	65
CHAPTER 8	Truth Tables (Regular or Long Method)	78
CHAPTER 9	Natural Deduction: Four Implication Rules	92
CHAPTER 10	Truth Tables (Indirect or Short Method)	113

Bibliography   123

CHAPTER 1
Logic and the Components of Arguments

> In Chapter 1, we will discuss the basic components of arguments, types of inductive arguments, and the strength and cogency of inductive reasoning.
> - Define the parts of an argument (premise vs. conclusion)
> - Identify premise or conclusion indicator words
> - Recognize the types of inductive arguments
> - Evaluate the strength and cogency of inductive reasoning

Although we are all equally entitled to hold our opinions, not all opinions are equally reasonable. Some are more sophisticated, well-supported by the evidence, and logically structured. When communicated clearly and persuasively, such opinions can have a lasting and profound impact on how we make decisions and conduct our lives. On the other hand, opinions based on lucky guesses, superstitions, wishful thinking, and faulty logic can often lead to a myriad of problems and negative consequences. Critical thinking and logic teach us how to draw conclusions based on evidence and good reasoning. They offer us tools to help us understand and evaluate reasoning whether it be our own or someone else's.

The focus of critical thinking and logic is on arguments. An argument is an attempt to support a statement by giving reasons for believing it. A single **argument** consists of a set of statements, one of which is the conclusion and the rest are the premises. The **conclusion** is the statement that someone is trying to convince others to believe, whereas the **premises** are the reasons offered in support of the conclusion. For many arguments, key words are contained in the passages to help distinguish the premises from the conclusion. **Conclusion indicator words** are placed near the conclusion of an argument to emphasize that it is the main point that the arguer is trying to persuade others. Conclusion indicators such as the words "therefore" or "consequently" point out that the conclusion of the argument is nearby.

> **Conclusion Indicators**
> therefore, thus, it follows that, consequently, in short, whence, we may infer, hence, so, accordingly, wherefore, entails that, implies that, as a result, we may conclude
>
> **Premise Indicators**
> since, because, for, as, due to, given that, seeing that, in view of, for the reason that, after all, inasmuch as, owing to, as evidenced by, in that, after all, considering that

Premise indicator words can alert us to the reasons offered in an argument. Words such as "since" or "because" often precede a premise. These indicator words can help us to determine which statements are intended to serve as the reasons in support of the conclusion. Sometimes an argument may not contain indicator words. In these cases, to identify the conclusion, we must then ask the following questions: What is the main point of the passage? What is the arguer trying to prove? What complicates things even more is that an argument's conclusion or one or more of its reasons may not be directly stated as an **explicit premise**. We then must interpret what the arguer is saying and determine what the **implicit premises** are. What is being said between the lines? What has the arguer implied but not explicitly stated?

In one of Sir Arthur Conan Doyle's stories, "Silver Blaze," Sherlock Holmes solves the mystery of the missing famous racehorse. Holmes concluded that the horse had not been abducted by a stranger; otherwise, the watchdog would have barked. The argument would look something like this:

> The racehorse was stolen in the night. **Considering that** watchdogs bark at strangers, and the dog did not bark, **it follows that** the racehorse was not stolen by a stranger.

The premises and conclusion of Sherlock's argument are easy to detect because of the indicator words "considering that" and "it follows that," which point out the premises and conclusion.

The presence of words such as "thus" or "because" does not automatically mean that a certain passage contains an argument. For example, the following passage is best interpreted as illustrating rather than arguing a point.

> Treat those who are good with goodness, and also treat those who are not good with goodness. Thus, goodness is attained. Be honest to those who are honest and be also honest to those who are not honest. Thus, honesty is attained. (Lao Tzu)

In this context, the word "thus" does not act as a conclusion indicator word because the passage is not an argument. It is illustrating how something is done rather than supporting the truth of a statement based on reasons. The Daoist sage, Lao Tzu, is trying to show how goodness and honesty are attained and uses the word "thus" to mean "in this way" or "in this manner."

In the next passage, the word "because" does not act as a premise indicator word in an argument. This passage contains an explanation. People may confuse arguments with explanations. An argument aims to prove that a certain claim is true based on reasons, while an explanation tries to show why something happens. It is meant to shed light on a certain event. In the following passage, Joseph Campbell is explaining how fear and desire prevent one from having certain experiences; he is not offering proof that this sort of experience is real.

> The experience of mystery comes not from expecting it but through yielding all your programs, because your programs are based on fear and desire. Drop them and the radiance comes. (Joseph Campbell, *Thou Art That: Transforming Religious Metaphor*)

To contain an argument, a passage must draw an inference that a certain conclusion follows from alleged facts or reasons. When giving an argument, a person is making two claims. The first is a **factual claim**. The premises of an argument offer support or evidence. Second, an **inferential claim** is being made that the truth of another statement (i.e., the conclusion) follows from the premises. That is, the arguer contends that the premises imply or entail the truth of the conclusion. Whether the premises indeed provide adequate support for the conclusion is another matter related to the strength or validity of the argument.

Exercise 1-A Identify Premises and Conclusion

Directions: All of these passages contain an argument. Underline the conclusion of each argument and circle any premise or conclusion indicator words.

1. Since all rational beings are responsible for their actions, and since all human beings are rational, it follows that all human beings are responsible for their actions.
2. Jones does not attend church. After all, he is an atheist, and atheists do not attend church.
3. It's not a good idea to drink five shots of Tequila. For you are likely to wake up with a big hangover.
4. Bombing the village caused great suffering. The pilot should not have done it.
5. The house across the street has shown no signs of life for several days. Some rain-soaked newspapers lie on the front steps. The grass badly needs cutting. The people across the street thus must be away on a trip.
6. Australia is either north or south of the equator. Due to the fact that Australia is not north of the equator, it must be south of the equator.
7. Smith ought to exercise more. Smith is overweight, and he has a heart condition. Also, exercise would give him a more positive outlook on life.
8. Taking a logic class can help students learn how to think critically. Logic also helps to develop strategic planning and complex problem-solving. Furthermore, it can aid those who plan to take the LSAT or GRE. In short, taking a logic class is a good idea for students.
9. Scientists used to claim that our solar system has nine planets. Since Pluto is no longer considered a planet, it follows that scientists think that there are eight planets in our solar system.

10. Lying is not a wise move. If you are found out, you probably will be in more trouble than if you had told the truth. Also, people may doubt your word in the future.
11. There are no foxes in this area. For we haven't seen one all day.
12. Bill should not marry the woman. She is a high school dropout; she is a recovering drug addict; furthermore, she is rumored to be an ex-prostitute!
13. Everyone in the chemistry class needed to have had one year of high school chemistry as a prerequisite. Given that John is a member of that class, he should have had one year of high school chemistry.
14. The fact that many drug addicts admit that they started on marijuana implies that marijuana causes addiction to hard drugs.
15. Since Hesperus is Venus, and Phosphorus is Venus, it follows that Hesperus is Phosphorus.
16. A Mustang convertible is the car for me! After all, rock star Jay Cool drives one.
17. In order for a democracy to function properly, it is necessary that the people have their voice heard. Given that the best way for the people's voice to be heard is through the process of voting, everyone should participate in the voting procedures.
18. Just as the body bears the traces of its phylogenetic development, so also does the human mind. Hence, there is nothing surprising about the possibility that the figurative language of dreams is a survival from an archaic mode of thought. (Carl Jung)
19. Neither a borrower nor a lender be, for loan oft loses both itself and friend. (William Shakespeare)
20. You have enemies? Good. That means you've stood up for something, sometime in your life. (Winston Churchill)

Induction, Strength, and Cogency

Rhetorical devices and fallacious reasoning can be effective tools of persuasion, but they do not make for good arguments. As previously stated, an **argument** is an attempt to support a statement by giving reasons for believing it. An argument consists of a set of statements, one of which is the conclusion, and the rest are the premises. The statement being argued for is the argument's conclusion. The premises are the statements that provide the data, evidence, or principles offered in support of the conclusion. The premises and the conclusion of an argument are special kinds of sentences called **statements**. A statement is a sentence that has a **truth-value** (i.e., it is either true or false). Your English teacher will refer to these as declarative sentences because they make assertions or claims. Unlike other sentences such as questions

Types of Inductive Arguments
Prediction: conclusion about future events based on past or present events
Authority: conclusion based on the testimony of others, typically experts
Causal Inference: conclusion based on a cause-effect relationship
Generalization: conclusion about a larger group from a smaller sample
Analogy: conclusion based on a similarity between two different objects

or commands, a statement is a sentence with a truth-value; it is either true or false. Questions such as "What time is it?" or commands such as "Stand up" have no truth-values, for they are neither true nor false.

Arguments may be divided into two broad groups, **deductive** and **inductive**. One way to differentiate deductive from inductive arguments is to point out the kind of reasoning involved in these two types of arguments. Inductive arguments contain or claim to contain probabilistic reasoning, whereas deductive arguments contain or claim to contain necessary reasoning. For inductive arguments, the premise(s) is intended to provide probable support for the conclusion. That is, based on the information given in the premises, one may believe that the conclusion of a good inductive argument is likely to be true. Certain argument forms are typically categorized as inductive because they have the potential of giving probable support for the conclusion. These inductive argument forms include predictions, arguments from authority, causal inferences, generalizations, and analogies.

In another story, "The Red-Headed League," Sherlock Holmes grows suspicious of the new assistant of the redheaded pawnbroker. This assistant, Vincent Spaulding, offered to work for only half the usual salary and spent a lot of time in the basement of the pawnshop. After a month working at the pawnshop, Spaulding convinces the pawnbroker to apply for a high-paying position advertised in the paper, a part-time job calling for a redhead to work four hours straight. Later, Sherlock stops by the pawnshop and notices that Spaulding's pants were stained at the knees, and the ground near the pawnshop was hollow. From these facts, Holmes predicts that a bank robbery was about to take place, perpetrated by the notorious criminal, John Clay, alias Vincent Spaulding. For weeks, the assistant had been tunneling his way from the pawnshop to the nearby bank. The temporary employment of the pawnbroker was just a ruse so that John Clay could dig the tunnel undetected.

Sherlock employed inductive reasoning to solve the case. The detective observed the proximity of the bank to the pawnshop and the hollowness of the ground. From these facts, he inferred the motive behind the assistant's unusual behavior, as well as the cause of the stains on his pants. Consequently, Sherlock was able to prevent a bank robbery after making strong causal inferences.

Inductive arguments are evaluated as being either strong or weak, and either cogent or uncogent. At the most general level, we understand an argument to be good if it provides support for a particular claim. In logic, instead of simply calling inductive arguments "good" or "bad," we will rate arguments by more specific evaluative terms. One way an inductive argument can be good is by being strong. An inductive argument is said to be **strong** just in case the conclusion is probably true given the premises. In other words, an argument is strong if, whenever all its premises are assumed to be true, the conclusion is unlikely to be false. For a strong argument, the truth of the premises makes the truth of the conclusion highly

Strong
If all the premises are assumed true, then the conclusion is PROBABLY true.

Cogent
(1) It is a strong argument, and (2) all the premises are true.

probable or likely but cannot guarantee certainty. In an informal sense, you may say that the conclusion of a strong argument must follow with probability from its premises. An argument that is intended to be strong, but is not, is **weak**.

Inductive arguments may also be evaluated as cogent or uncogent. An argument is **cogent** if it is strong and all its premises are true. Thus, for cogent arguments, two conditions are required: the conclusion probably follows from the premises, and all the premises are true. Given the definition of strength, it follows that a cogent argument has a probably true conclusion. Such a conclusion is most likely true but may possibly be false. An argument is uncogent if any of its premises are false or if it is weak. Let us consider a few examples. The truth-values of the statements are indicated in parentheses.

Example One
(strong, cogent)
Most dogs bark at strangers (T).
The dog did not bark at the thief (T).
The dog knew the thief (T).

Example Two
(weak, uncogent)
Sherlock Holmes is a detective (T).
Watson is the friend of Holmes (T).
Sherlock Holmes smokes a pipe (T).

Example Three
(strong, uncogent)
Most workers accept half pay (F).
Spaulding works at the pawnshop (T).
Spaulding accepts half pay (T).

Example Four
(weak, uncogent)
Some people hire Sherlock Holmes (T).
Some employers hire redheads (T).
Sherlock Holmes is a redhead (F).

In Examples One and Three, all the premises have to be true for the argument to be cogent; however, for an argument to be strong, not all of the premises must be true. Example Two shows how an inductive argument may contain all true statements but can still fail to be strong. This is because the strength of an argument concerns the relationship between the premises and the conclusion. Although the premises and conclusion of Example Two are true, the premises are not inferentially linked to the conclusion. That is, being a detective and having Watson as a friend will not lead us to believe that Holmes probably smokes a pipe. In Example Four, the premises, while true, provide insufficient evidence to prove the conclusion that Holmes is a redhead. Thus, Example Four is weak, and whenever an argument is weak, it is automatically uncogent regardless of the truth-values of the premises.

An inductive argument can be strong even if all the statements are false, as the following example illustrates.

Example Five
(strong, uncogent)
Most pawnbrokers are redheaded (F).

Dr. Watson is a pawnbroker (F).
Dr. Watson is redheaded (F).

Although both premises and the conclusion are false, the argument nevertheless is strong because if the two premises were true, the conclusion would probably be true. It is uncogent because not all premises are in fact true, at least according to the Sherlock Holmes stories. Thus, when evaluating an argument as strong or weak, begin by assuming or pretending that all the premises are true. Then ask whether the conclusion would probably be true based on those assumptions. A strong argument is one in which the conclusion would probably be true if one pretended that the premises were true. After that, label all weak arguments uncogent. Strong arguments with true premises are cogent, while strong arguments with at least one false premise are uncogent.

There are three possibilities for inductive arguments: (1) strong, cogent; (2) strong, uncogent; and (3) weak, uncogent.

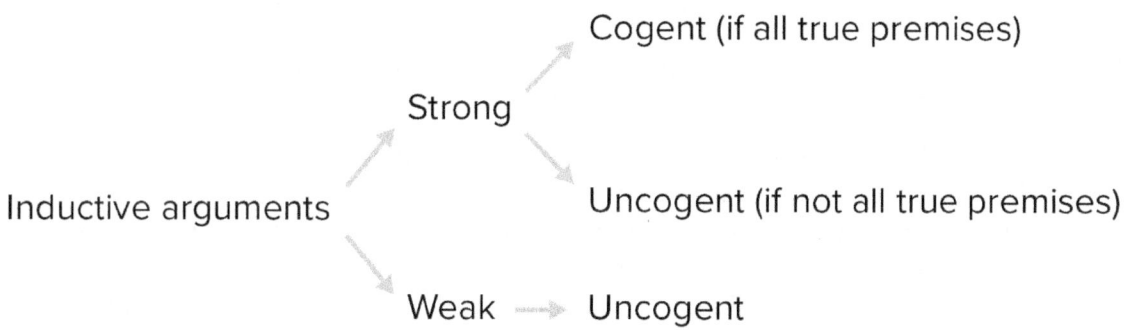

Furthermore, it is important to note that the terms "strong" and "weak" refer to arguments, not to statements. We may call an argument strong or weak, and cogent or uncogent. However, we will not claim that a statement is strong or weak; rather, a statement has a truth-value and is either true or false. Also, inductive arguments can vary in levels of strength and weakness. Compare the following two strong and cogent arguments:

Example Six
(strong, uncogent)
Holmes solves 95 percent of his cases (F).
Holmes will solve his next case (T).

Example Seven
(strong, uncogent)
Holmes solves 80 percent of his cases (F).
Holmes will solve his next case (T).

Example Six is a stronger argument than Example Seven based on the percentages, 95 percent versus 80 percent, making the probability of a true conclusion more likely given the premises.

Unlike deductive arguments, inductive arguments assert that the conclusion is probably true and not necessarily true. The following two arguments are both cogent arguments, although the conclusion of Example Eight is true while the conclusion of Example Nine is false. Thus, the conclusion of a cogent argument does not have to be true but may actually be false. What is important is that the conclusion is likely to be true given the premises. Although the conclusion of a cogent argument is probably true based on the premises, it is still possible that the conclusion is false.

Example Eight
(strong, cogent)
Holmes solves most of his cases (T).
Holmes solved the case of
"The Red-Headed League" (T).

Example Nine
(strong, cogent)
Holmes solves most of his cases (T).
Holmes solved the case of
"A Scandal in Bohemia" (F).

Exercise 1-B Evaluate Inductive Arguments

Determine whether the inductive argument is strong or weak, and cogent or uncogent. The truth-values of the premises are indicated in parentheses.

1. Ray Charles and Stevie Wonder are musicians (T). They are both blind (T). This means that the majority of musicians are blind.
2. The parking enforcement officer told me that the parking meter was out of order (T). So, the meter is probably not working.
3. The fortune teller looked into her crystal ball and said that I would have a long and happy life (T). Accordingly, I anticipate a long and happy life ahead of me.
4. Sue must have gone to the beach because her swimsuit is wet (T), and her shoes are full of sand (T).
5. No one would blame a bartender for having a few drinks on the job (T). But an airline pilot is no less a human being than a bartender (T). Therefore, no one should blame an airline pilot for having a few drinks on the job.
6. Lassie, Benji, and Rin Tin Tin are all dogs that have been in the movies (T). Hence, it follows that most dogs are movie stars.
7. My math teacher said that an octagon has eight sides (T). Thus, it must be the case that an octagon has eight sides.
8. There are mushrooms growing in my front lawn (F). They look like the kind of mushrooms I buy from the grocery store (T). Therefore, they are probably healthy and delicious to eat.
9. Some dogs have rabies and bite little children (T). It follows that most dogs are dangerous and vicious.
10. The brownies that Jan baked are burnt to a crisp (F). She must have left them in the oven for too long.
11. Most Europeans are South Americans (F). Jean is European (T). So, Jean is South American.

12. Larry is Joe's friend (F). Joe is Tina's friend (F). It follows that Tina is probably Larry's friend.
13. Kevin likes Julia (T). Julia likes David (F). Consequently, Kevin probably likes David.
14. Rita is looking at Fred (T). Fred is looking at Jody (T). So, it is likely that Rita is looking at Jody.
15. Ninety-five percent of the people born in California are Native American Indians (F). Joe was born in California (F). So, it is likely that Joe is a Native American Indian.
16. Ninety percent of farm animals are pigs (F). Oliver is a pig (T). So, Oliver is probably a farm animal.
17. Most fish can swim (T). Porcupines are fish (F). So, porcupines can probably swim.
18. Most birds can fly (T). Penguins are birds (T). So, penguins can fly.
19. Most birds can fly (T). Penguins can fly (F). So, penguins are birds.
20. Most journalists are good writers (T). Bart is a journalist (T). Thus, Bart is a good writer.
21. Ninety-five percent of all Yugoslavians are acrobats (F). Jane Fonda is Yugoslavian (F). Therefore, Jane Fonda is probably an acrobat.
22. All U.S. presidents have been men (T). Frank Sinatra is a man (T). Therefore, the next US president will probably be Frank Sinatra.
23. Most birds can fly (T). Butterflies can fly (T). Therefore, butterflies are birds.
24. Most flying things are birds (F). Butterflies can fly (T). So, butterflies are birds.
25. Most cats have four legs (T). Scott has a cat (T). So, his cat has four legs.
26. Eighty percent of dogs are golden retrievers (F). Thus, Lassie is a golden retriever.

Exercise 1-C Identify Inductive Argument Form

For the first ten problems of Exercise 2-A, identify the inductive argument form: prediction, argument from authority, causal inference, inductive generalization, or analogy.

Exercise 1-D True or False Questions

Answer "true" or "false" to the following statements:
1. The question "What time is it?" is a statement.
2. The words "therefore," "hence," and "since," are all conclusion indicators.
3. The words "because," "for," and "after all" are all premise indicator words.
4. An analogy draws a conclusion about a future event based on our knowledge of similar events.
5. The conclusion of an inductive argument is necessarily true.
6. "Five is an even number" is a statement with a truth-value.
7. All statements have a truth-value.

8. An inductive argument must have two premises and one conclusion.
9. A causal inference draws a conclusion about a whole group from a smaller sample.
10. A prediction is a type of inductive argument.
11. All inductive generalizations are strong arguments.
12. Some arguments from authority can be weak.
13. All inductive generalizations are strong arguments.
14. All cogent inductive arguments are strong.
15. All strong arguments have a true conclusion.
16. A cogent argument may have a false conclusion.
17. A strong argument may be uncogent.
18. A weak argument must be uncogent.
19. An inductive argument with false premises must be uncogent.
20. A strong argument must have true premises.
21. A cogent argument must have true premises.
22. An argument that contains only true statements must be strong.
23. A strong argument with a false conclusion must be uncogent.
24. An argument may legitimately be described as true.
25. All strong, cogent arguments have probably true conclusions.

CHAPTER 2
Deduction, Validity, and Soundness

> In Chapter 2, we will focus on deductive reasoning, the types of deductive arguments, and the validity and soundness of deductive reasoning.
> - Identify the types of deductive arguments
> - Evaluate the validity and soundness of deductive reasoning
> - Distinguish between common invalid and valid argument forms

We shall now shift our focus to deductive arguments. As previously mentioned, **deductive** arguments contain or claim to contain necessary reasoning, whereas inductive arguments contain or claim to contain probabilistic reasoning. For deductive arguments, the premises are intended to provide the necessary support for the conclusion. The best deductive arguments do not merely assure us that the conclusion is probably true based on the premises but that the conclusion is guaranteed to be true.

When deciding whether an argument is best treated as an inductive or a deductive argument, one should first consider how good the argument is. If the premises of the argument provide the necessary support for the conclusion, then the argument is deductive. On the other hand, if the argument is good but its premises provide only probable support for the conclusion, then the argument is inductive.

Can we classify bad arguments as deductive or inductive? For, some arguments are not good in the sense that they neither provide necessary nor probable support for the conclusion. When the argument is bad, we can still determine whether to treat it as a deductive argument rather than an inductive argument, or vice versa. First, the presence of indicator words such as *probably*, *likely*, *certainly*, *necessarily* can give us a clue about how best to categorize the argument. Second, some types of argument forms are typically associated with inductive reasoning, while others are associated with deductive reasoning. The inductive argument forms include prediction, analogy, generalization, causal inference,

> **Types of Deductive Arguments**
>
> **Argument from definition:** argument based on a definition of a word or phrase
>
> **Argument from math:** argument based on a mathematical principle
>
> **Categorical Syllogism:** argument with two premises and a conclusion, and each sentence begins with the word "all" "no" or "some"
>
> **Disjunctive Syllogism:** argument with two premises and a conclusion, and one of the premises is a disjunctive statement (Either A or B)
>
> **Hypothetical Syllogism:** argument with two premises and a conclusion, and at least one of the premises is a conditional statement (If A, then B)

and argument from authority. In this chapter, we will focus on these deductive argument forms: argument from math, argument from definition, categorical syllogism, disjunctive syllogism, and hypothetical syllogism.

A syllogism is a special type of deductive argument that contains exactly two premises and one conclusion. The different types of syllogisms are easy to recognize by the kinds of statements included in them. A categorical syllogism is a deductive argument containing categorical claims, sentences that begin with the words "all," "no," or "some." We will specify other requirements for a categorical syllogism in a later chapter. These are some examples of categorical syllogisms:

All canoes are boats.
Some rafts are not boats.
So, no rafts are canoes.

Some buildings are skyscrapers.
No skyscrapers are huts.
Some huts are not buildings.

Two other kinds of syllogisms are disjunctive syllogisms and hypothetical syllogisms. These syllogisms will contain special compound statements whose truth-values are a function of the simpler statements contained in them. In disjunctive syllogisms, one of the premises is a disjunctive statement of the form "Either A or B." In hypothetical syllogisms, at least one of the premises is a conditional statement of the form "If A, then B."

1. **Disjunctive Statement** (EITHER A OR B) – For a disjunctive statement to be true, only one of the component simple statements need be true. The disjunct A can be true, disjunct B can be true, or both A and B can be true. For example, "Jane is happy or excited" is a true disjunction when one or both of its component statements "Jane is happy" or "Jane is excited" is true.
2. **Conditional Statement** (IF A, THEN B) – For a conditional, the first part is identified as the **antecedent** and the second part as the **consequent**. A conditional is true except for the case when its antecedent A is true, and its consequent B is false. For example, "If it is September, then it is winter" is a conditional statement. This conditional statement is false when the antecedent "it is September" is true while the consequent "it is winter" is false.

Disjunctive Syllogism	Hypothetical Syllogism
Either the number 12 is odd or even.	If the vase fell, then it broke.
The number 12 is not odd.	The vase fell.
So, the number 12 is even.	Therefore, the vase broke.

Arguments categorized as deductive may or may not be good arguments. For example, there can be good syllogisms as well as bad ones. Deductive reasoning may be fallacious and thereby not offer a necessarily true conclusion. The two examples of categorical syllogisms are both bad deductive arguments. In contrast to the good disjunctive and hypothetical syllogisms in the previous examples, we can create some bad deductive arguments with a few modifications:

Disjunctive Syllogism	Hypothetical Syllogism
Either the number 11 is odd or even.	If the vase fell, then it broke.
The number 11 is not odd.	The vase broke.
So, the number 11 is even.	Therefore, the vase fell.

There may also be good arguments from math, as well as bad ones. Good mathematical arguments are ones in which the arguer supports a conclusion based on correct mathematical principles and accurate data. Some calculations may be erroneous due to faulty measurements, wrong formulas, or misapplied mathematics. In these cases, instead of saying that such arguments are not arguments from math, we will simply categorize these defective arguments as arguments from math but evaluate them as bad ones. Similarly, when a person misunderstands the actual meaning of a word or phrase, arguments by definition may be failed attempts to support a conclusion. Nevertheless, we would still treat these arguments by definition as bad examples of deductive reasoning. So, it is important to emphasize that a deductive argument is one in which the arguer claims to be providing necessary support for a conclusion. When the arguer succeeds in doing this, then we have a deductive argument that we can evaluate as being a good one.

Evaluating Deductive Arguments

At the most general level, we call an argument good if it can provide reasons to believe a particular claim, the conclusion. Just as we had for inductive arguments, we will rate deductive arguments using specific evaluative terms. We will evaluate deductive arguments by the terms valid or invalid, and sound or unsound.

VALID → IF all the premises are assumed true, THEN the conclusion must be true.

SOUND → (1) it is a valid argument, AND
(2) all the premises are true

One way a deductive argument can be good is by being valid. An argument is **valid** if and only if the conclusion is necessarily true given the premises. That is, the premises provide undeniable support for the conclusion. More casually, you may say that the conclusion of a valid argument must follow from its premises. Validity concerns the relationship between the premises and the conclusion, and not the actual truth-values of the component statements at all. The premises do not all have to be true for an argument to be valid. Validity also does not guarantee a true conclusion, but if all the premises of a valid argument are true, then the conclusion would be true. Thus, the only truth-value combination not possible for valid arguments is one where all the premises are true while the conclusion is false. Furthermore, it is important to note that the term "valid" applies to arguments, not to statements. An argument that is not valid is called invalid. Statements are not said to be "valid" or "invalid"; rather, statements are legitimately said to be "true" or "false."

The best kind of deductive argument is not only valid, but it is also sound. An argument is **sound** if and only if it is valid and all its premises are true. That means that the conclusion necessarily follows from the premises and that all the premises are true. Not only does a sound argument have true premises, but given the definition of validity, it follows that a sound argument always has a true conclusion. Example One is a sound argument because it meets the two requirements of being valid and having all true premises. An argument is unsound if any of its premises are false or if it is not valid.

Example One
(valid, sound)
All dogs are mammals. (T)
Lassie is a dog. (T)
So, Lassie is a mammal. (T)

Example Two
(valid, unsound)
All dogs are reptiles. (F)
Shamu is a dog. (F)
So, Shamu is a reptile. (F)

Examples One and Two are both valid because if one were to assume the truth of the premises, then the conclusion would necessarily be true. To test for validity, begin by pretending that all the premises are true and then determine whether the conclusion would have to be true based on your assumptions. Consider Example Two: if you pretend that all dogs are reptiles and that Shamu is a dog, would it necessarily follow from these statements that Shamu is a reptile? The answer would be yes; it is a valid argument. We can compare these valid arguments to the next two examples of invalid arguments.

Example Three
(invalid, unsound)
All dogs are mammals. (T)
Lassie is a dog. (T)
So, Shamu is a killer whale. (T)

Example Four
(invalid, unsound)
All dogs are amphibians. (F)
Shamu is an amphibian. (F)
So, Shamu is a dog. (F)

For Examples Three and Four, the conclusion does not follow from the information given in the premises. Even though all the statements in Example Three are true (all dogs are mammals, Lassie is a dog, and Shamu is a killer whale), it is not a valid argument because the conclusion is not logically supported by the premises.

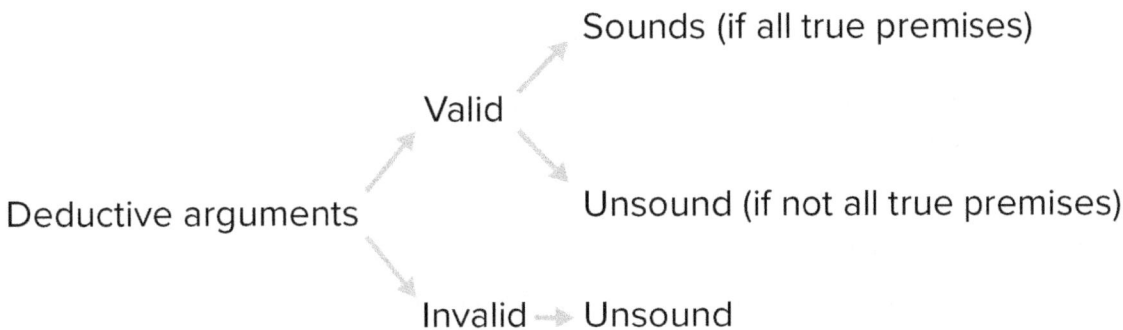

As shown in the diagram, all invalid arguments are unsound. On the other hand, a valid argument may be sound or unsound depending on the truth-values of the premises. Valid arguments with true premises are sound, while valid arguments with at least one false premise are unsound.

Thus, we see that the evaluative terms for deductive arguments correspond to the evaluative terms for inductive arguments. That is, validity and soundness for deductive arguments are similar to strength and cogency for inductive arguments. Whereas the conclusion of a strong inductive argument is probably true given the premises, the conclusion of a valid deductive argument is necessarily true if one assumed that the premises were true. Also, just as a cogent inductive argument must be a strong argument with all true premises, a sound deductive argument must be valid with all true premises.

There are special deductive argument forms related to **disjunctive syllogisms** and **hypothetical syllogisms**. We will now turn to deductive argument forms, which because of their form or structure are always valid or invalid. Some valid argument forms are so common and distinctive in logical discourse that they have been given special names such as modus ponens or modus tollens. Furthermore, some invalid arguments are defective in their structure and constitute formal fallacies. These include the formal fallacies of affirming the consequent and denying the antecedent.

Although the valid inference modus ponens looks very similar to the formal fallacy of affirming the consequent, they may be distinguished by the premises. If one of the premises is the antecedent of a conditional statement, then the argument is valid and commits modus ponens. If the one of the premises is the consequent, then the argument is invalid and commits affirming the consequent since one of its premises affirms the truth of the consequent.

VALID ARGUMENT FORMS

Disjunctive Syllogism (DS)
1. A or B
2. Not A
3. B

Modus Ponens (MP)
1. If A, then B
2. A
3. B

(sometimes this is called simply "Hypothetical Syllogism" or HS)

Chain Argument or (HS)
1. If A, then B
2. If B, then C
3. If A, then C

Modus Tollens (MT)
1. If A, then B
2. Not B
3. Not A

INVALID ARGUMENT FORMS

Affirming the Consequent (AC)
1. If A, then B
2. B
3. A

Denying the Antecedent (DA)
1. If A, then B
2. Not A
3. Not B

Example of Affirming the Consequent

If I am in San Diego, then I am in California. I am in California. Thus, I am in San Diego. This is invalid because the premises could be true, yet I may not be in San Diego. I could be in Sacramento, for example.

If the diver went swimming, then her swimsuit is wet. The diver's swimsuit is wet. Thus, the diver went swimming. This is invalid because the diver's swimsuit may be wet for other reasons (e.g., rain).

Examples of Denying the Antecedent

If I am in San Diego, then I am in California. I am not in San Diego. Therefore, I am not in California. I could still be in California, although I am not in San Diego.

If the diver went swimming, then her swimsuit is wet. The diver did not go swimming. So, her swimsuit is not wet.

For this last example of denying the antecedent, can you think of a scenario where the premises are both true while the conclusion is false? If so, then you have provided a counterexample and shown this argument to be invalid.

Exercise 2-A Evaluate Deductive Arguments

For each deductive argument determine whether the argument is valid or invalid and sound or unsound. The truth-values of the premises are indicated in parentheses. If the argument is a hypothetical syllogism, indicate whether it exemplifies modus ponens, modus tollens, fallacies of affirming the consequent, or denying the antecedent.

1. All violinists are South Americans (F). Rita is a violinist (T). So, Rita is South American.
2. No marsupials are amphibians (T). All koalas are marsupials (T). Hence, no koalas are amphibians.
3. Larry is Joe's friend (T). Joe is Tina's friend (F). Thus, Tina is certainly Larry's friend.
4. Jean can use her left hand and right hand with equal skill (F). So, she must be ambidextrous.
5. Either tomatoes are fruits or vegetables (T). Tomatoes are not vegetables (T). Consequently, tomatoes are fruits.
6. Since some pets are cats (T), and some pets are dogs (T), it follows that some pets are hamsters.
7. All men are mortal (T). Socrates is a man (T). Therefore, Socrates is mortal.
8. Odd numbers are divisible by two (F). Twelve is an odd number (F). Therefore, it must be the case that 12 is divisible by 2.
9. The radius of this circle is 2 inches (T). The circumference of a circle is $2\Pi r$ (T). Accordingly, the circumference of the circle is 2Π inches.
10. If you eat fast food, then you will be taking in more calories than you should (T). If you take in more calories than you need, then you will gain weight (T). Therefore, if you eat fast food, then you will gain weight.
11. If Napoleon is French, then Napoleon is a European (T). Napoleon is not French (F). So, it follows that Napoleon is not European.
12. If Napoleon is French, then Napoleon is European (T). Napoleon is French (T). Hence, Napoleon is European.
13. The sum of 5 and 7 is 12 (T). The sum of two odd numbers must be odd (F). Five and 7 are odd numbers (T). It follows that 12 is an odd number.
14. An octagon has six sides (F). The sign in front of my house is octagonal (F). Accordingly, the sign in front of my house has six sides.
15. Since James's birthday occurs before Grace's birthday (T), and Grace's birthday occurs after Anna's birthday (F), it follows that James's birthday occurs before Anna's birthday.
16. Either I had tacos or a burrito for lunch (T). I didn't have tacos (T). Therefore, I had a burrito.
17. Peter is belligerent (F). This implies that Peter is warlike or aggressive.
18. If Tony is from New York, then he is an American (T). Tony is an American (T). Therefore, Tony is from New York.
19. If I go to the concert, I won't wake up for school on time (F). I won't go to the concert (F). Therefore, I will wake up on time for school.

20. The Pentagon Building is triangular (F). Triangles have five sides (F). Therefore, the Pentagon Building has five sides.
21. Either you vote or don't vote (T). If you vote, you are exercising your right as a citizen (T). If you don't vote, you are wasting your right as a citizen (T). Therefore, you are either exercising or wasting your right as a citizen.
22. All koalas are amphibians (F). All amphibians are crustaceans (F). Thus, all koalas are crustaceans.
23. If Spot is a dog, then Spot is a mammal (T). Spot is not a mammal (T). So, Spot is not a dog.
24. The lengths of the sides of a rectangle are 5 inches and 10 inches (T). Therefore, the area of the rectangle is 15 inches.
25. The kids in school are hyper today (F). So, they must be overactive and have a hard time keeping still.
26. If Stalin was Swedish, then Stalin was a dictator (F). Stalin was not Swedish (T). So, it follows that Stalin was not a dictator.
27. Greg is taller than Sue (F). Sue is taller than Laura (T). Thus, Greg is taller than Laura.
28. Dolores is meticulous (T). This means Dolores is very detail-oriented and precise.
29. If Ted is baking cookies, then he needs flour (T). Ted does not need flour (T). Hence, Ted is not baking cookies.
30. Either Pam is a teacher or a nurse (F). Pam is not a teacher (T). Consequently, Pam is not a nurse.

Exercise 2-B Identify Deductive Argument Form

For the problems in Exercise 2-A, identify the type of deductive argument form (math, definition, categorical, disjunctive, or hypothetical syllogism). In some cases, the argument may be deductive but may not fit one of these five forms.

Exercise 2-C True or False Questions

1. A deductive argument must have two premises and one conclusion.
2. The following is an argument from a definition: Cholesterol is endogenous with humans. Therefore, it is manufactured inside the human body.
3. Disjunctive syllogisms contain a statement of the form "Either … or. …"
4. All sound deductive arguments are valid.
5. All deductive arguments have a necessarily true conclusion.
6. Some invalid arguments are sound.
7. A sound argument may have a false conclusion.
8. A valid argument must have a true conclusion.

9. If an argument has true premises and a true conclusion, we know that it is a perfectly good argument.
10. A statement may legitimately be spoken of as "valid" or "invalid."
11. A chain argument consists of three conditional statements.
12. In the statement "If X, then Y," the antecedent is X.
13. Affirming the consequent is a valid deductive argument form.
14. Denying the antecedent is an invalid deductive argument form.
15. Modus ponens is an invalid deductive argument form.
16. A hypothetical syllogism contains at least one conditional statement.
17. The chain argument is a type of hypothetical syllogism.
18. Modus tollens is a type of hypothetical syllogism.
19. A modus tollens with all true premises must be sound.
20. A chain argument with a false premise must be invalid.

Exercise 2-D Deductive or Inductive

Determine whether the argument is best categorized as deductive or inductive.

1. Squirrels are like rabbits. Squirrels can climb trees. Likewise, rabbits are able to climb trees also.
2. All marathon runners are athletes. Stefano is a marathon runner. Accordingly, Stefano is a runner.
3. Frank is taller than Holly, and Holly is taller than Jack. Thus, Frank is taller than Jack.
4. The school bell rings daily at 7:00 a.m. Since it is 6:59 a.m., the bell will ring in one minute.
5. No children are adults, and some adults are senior citizens. It follows that some children are not senior citizens.
6. Betty looks ten years younger. She must have had plastic surgery!
7. Charlie either ordered a hamburger or a grilled cheese sandwich for lunch. He did not order a hamburger for lunch. So, he must have ordered a grilled cheese sandwich.
8. If Diana goes to the prom with Jason, then Bill goes to the prom with Tammy. Diana does not go to the prom with Jason. Therefore, Bill does not go to the prom with Tammy.
9. I met five of my brother's friends, and they were all introverted Goths. It follows that any friend of my brother is an introverted Goth.
10. Peter lied to Greta, and Greta lied to Jocelyn. Hence, Peter probably lied to Jocelyn.

CHAPTER 3
Categorical Reasoning

> In Chapter 3, we will learn about categorical reasoning, the different types of categorical statements, and the validity of immediate inferences.
> - Recognize categorical statements in standard form
> - Identify the parts, letter names, quantity, and quality of categorical statements
> - Use two-circle Venn diagrams to evaluate the validity of immediate inferences

In the present chapter, we will learn about Aristotelian logic, the first comprehensive system of logic formulized by the Greek philosopher Aristotle over 2,000 years ago. It is still a powerful tool today for analyzing arguments that contain categorical statements. A categorical statement expresses a relation between two classes of things, and typically begins with the word "all," "no," or "some."

Four Categorical Claims

Categorical claims, which make assertions about groups or categories of things, make up the subject matter of categorical logic. A **standard-form categorical claim** has one of these forms and each has a letter name: A, E, I, or O.

A: All _____ are _____.

E: No _____ are _____.

I: Some _____ are _____.

O: Some _____ are not _____.

Categorical claims have plural nouns or noun phrases in the above blanks. We call these nouns and noun phrases **terms**. The first term in a standard-form categorical claim is its **subject term**, S. The second is its **predicate term**, P. Each categorical claim begins with the **quantifier** "all," "no," or "some." The quantifier is a word that tells us how much of the subject term we are talking about. For example, the categorical statement, "Some primates are chimpanzees," relates to the class of primates with the class of chimpanzees. The word "some" acts as a quantifier, letting us know how much of the class of primates is included in the class of chimpanzees. The subject and predicate terms are joined by the **copula** "are" for A-, E-, and I-claims and by "are not" for O-claims.

Each of the four categorical claims can be given a visual illustration in a **Venn diagram**. In each Venn diagram, the two overlapping circles represent the groups or categories named by the subject and predicate term. A shaded area represents an empty class: the class or set contains no members. An area with an X represents a class that is not empty: the class or set contains at least one member. We shall first draw the Venn diagrams for categorical claims according to the Boolean viewpoint. Not agreeing fully with Aristotle, nineteenth-century British mathematician George Boole interpreted the four categorical statements as follows:

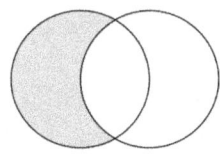
"All S are P" (A) means "The class of S outside of P is empty."

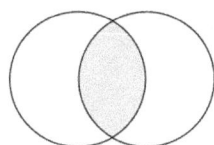
"No S are P" (E) means "The class of S inside P is empty."

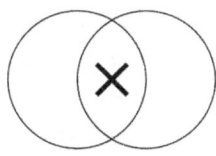
"Some S are P" (I) means "The class of S inside P has at least one member."

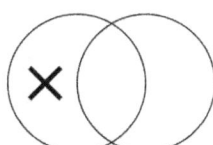
"Some S are not P" (O) means "The class of S outside of P has at least one member."

These four statements may be categorized into **affirmative** (**A** and **I**) and **negative** (**E** and **O**) claims. Affirmative and negative distinguish the **"quality"** of a categorical claim. Affirmative claims include one class within another; they contain no negation words. "All owls are birds" and "Some birds are parrots" are affirmative, asserting that members of the subject class are included in the predicate class. Negative claims exclude one class within another; they contain a negation word, "no" or "not." Affirmative claims affirm while negative claims deny class membership. "No whales are penguins" and "Some birds are not penguins" are negative, excluding all or some members of the subject class from the predicate class.

Categorical claims may also be classified according to their **"quantity."** **Universal** propositions assert something about every member of the S class. A and E statements are universal. For example, "all dogs are canines," and "no dogs are felines" make a claim about every member of the subject class, dogs. **Particular** propositions assert something about one or more members of the S class. I and O statements are particular in quantity. Only some members of the subject class, and not all members, are asserted to be included in or excluded from the predicate class in these examples: "Some people are acrobats" and "Some people are not ventriloquists."

Boole's interpretation of the four categorical claims is similar to Aristotle's with regard to I and O statements. Both Aristotle and Boole understand particular categorical statements to have existential import. The two statements "Some people are acrobats" and "Some people are not ventriloquists" cannot be true unless the subject term people refer to actually existing things. One statement asserts that there exists at least one person who is an acrobat, while the other asserts that there exists at least one person who is not a ventriloquist. Thus, particular statements I and O have existential import because they make positive claims about the existence of at least one member of the subject class.

Where Aristotle and Boole differ is in regard to A- and E-claims. Let us first consider A statements that begin with the quantifier "all."

All philosophers are rational creatures.

Aristotle takes the traditional approach and interprets this universal sentence as having existential import, for he assumes that "philosophers" refer to actually existing things. This sentence is true just in case every philosopher is a rational creature; it assumes that at least one philosopher exists. The Aristotelian interpretation is what we normally adopt in our everyday conversations since we usually assume that the subject that we are talking about actually exists. Boole does not make this existential assumption. Boole's interpretation of universal statements makes sense when we run across a statement such as this:

All unicorns are one-horned animals.

Boole states that sentences such as this show that universal statements do not necessarily have existential import. This sentence does not imply that unicorns exist at all. It may be interpreted hypothetically. That is, if there were such things as unicorns, then they would be one-horned animals. Thus, a universal statement beginning with "all" does not presuppose the existence of any members of its subject class. Similarly, when it comes to universal E statements beginning with "no," Aristotle takes the traditional approach, while Boole takes this modern stance.

No ghosts are corporeal creatures.

From the traditional Aristotelian interpretation, this sentence implies the existence of ghosts. Whereas from the Boolean standpoint, it has no existential import and may be interpreted hypothetically. For Boole, the sentence means: "If there were such things as ghosts, then they would not be corporeal creatures." In this way, the Boolean standpoint is neutral about existence. The Aristotelian and the Boolean interpretations do agree regarding particular statements. Particular statements that begin with the quantifier "some" do have existential import. Thus, "some tigers are ferocious" implies that there is at least one tiger, and that tiger is ferocious from both the Aristotelian and the Boolean standpoints.

With respect to Venn diagrams and the square of opposition, we will be combining both the Boolean and Aristotelian interpretations. In some cases, when the Aristotelian standpoint is not applicable, we will restrict ourselves only to the Boolean interpretation.

We can also draw the **negation** of categorical statements. Where we had marked an "X" for a categorical statement, we would shade the area to draw the negation. Where there was shading in an area, we would mark an "X" in order to express the negation.

For example, suppose someone were to tell you that "some whales are sharks." This person would have you believe that the following Venn diagram is true.

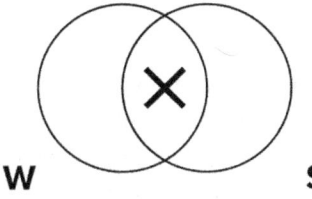

"Some W (whales) are S (sharks)."

However, this Venn diagram is inaccurate. In reality, there exists nothing which is both a whale and a shark, and so there should not be an X in the intersection of the Venn circles. You might respond that "It is false that some W are S." Instead of placing an X in the intersection, you would shade the intersection to express that nothing exists in the middle area. So, your Venn diagram for "It is false that some W are S."

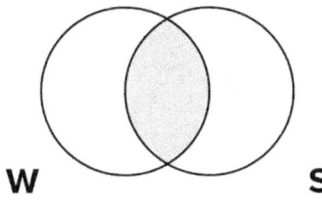

"It is false that Some W (whales) are S (sharks)."

To draw the negation of the statement "Some W are S," you simply change the X to shading. Simply by changing X's to shading or shading to X's, you can draw the negation of the categorical claims:

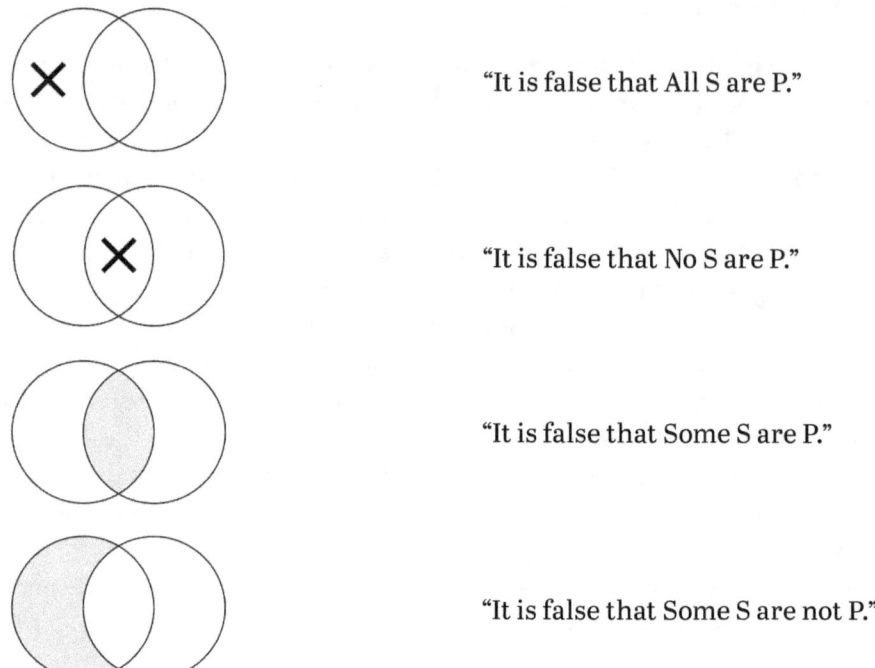

"It is false that All S are P."

"It is false that No S are P."

"It is false that Some S are P."

"It is false that Some S are not P."

Venn diagrams may be used to show the logical relationships among *corresponding* categorical claims. Two categorical claims **correspond** to one another when they have the same subject term and the same predicate term. As they stand, "All experts are professionals" and "Some professionals are not experts" do not correspond because the subject and predicate terms have switched places. When we have an argument with two corresponding categorical claims, we may draw Venn diagrams to determine the validity of **immediate inferences** (i.e., arguments that have one premise and one conclusion). We proceed by drawing the Venn diagram for the premise and for the conclusion and then compare the conclusion diagram with our premise diagram. When determining whether the argument is valid or invalid, we must consider whether the conclusion is necessarily true given the premise. In other words, if we assume the premise is true, would the conclusion have to be true?

Venn Diagram Method for Determining Validity of Immediate Inferences

1. First, begin by applying the Boolean standpoint.
2. Then, apply the Aristotelian standpoint to certain cases.

Let us consider this immediate inference and determine the validity of the argument using the two-circle Venn diagram method:

Example One:

<u>No guitars are drums.</u>
Therefore, it is false that some guitars are drums.

Let us start by drawing Venn diagrams from only the Boolean standpoint. The premise will be drawn in the top circles and the conclusion in the bottom circles. We should label the left circles as G for "guitars" and the right circles D for "drums."

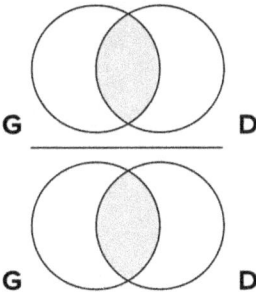

The intersection of the top premise circles is shaded because that is the standard way we draw E-claims that begin with "no"—we shade the middle section. For the conclusion, we have the negation of an I-claim "Some G are D." Without the negation expressed by "it is false that," we would mark an X in the middle of the bottom conclusion circles. But, since there is a negation, we understand the conclusion to say that it is false that there is an X in the middle, so we shade that area rather than draw an X. When deciding validity, we ask whether the conclusion is guaranteed by the premise. That is, is the conclusion necessarily true if we accept the information given by the premise? Indeed, if the middle area is empty as the premise circles show, then the conclusion would have to be true since it shows the very same thing—that the intersection is empty. Thus, this argument is valid from the Boolean standpoint.

Example Two:

<u>Some gypsies are not singers.</u>
Therefore, some gypsies are singers.

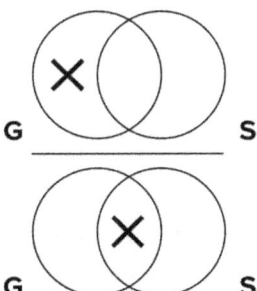

After labeling our left circles G after the subject term "gypsies" and the right circles S for the predicate term "singers," we draw X's in the appropriate sections for the O-claim and the I-claim. The premise circles show that there is something in the G circle outside of the S circle. If we assume the premise is true, we must ask ourselves whether it must necessarily be true that there is an X in the intersection of the two circles G and S. The answer is no. Just because there is something in one section does not guarantee that there is something in the middle area, as shown in the conclusion circles. Hence, since the conclusion does not necessarily follow, this argument is invalid. While the conclusion is possibly true, it is not necessarily true given the premise. These first two examples are complete by applying only the Boolean interpretation of categorical claims without the need of taking the Aristotelian standpoint.

Here are several more immediate inferences and Venn diagrams from the Boolean standpoint; however, for a couple of these arguments, we will need to apply the Aristotelian standpoint.

<u>All men are painters.</u>
Some men are painters.

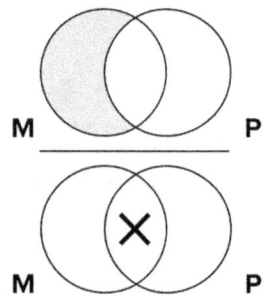

<u>It is false that all witches are ogres.</u>
Some witches are not ogres.

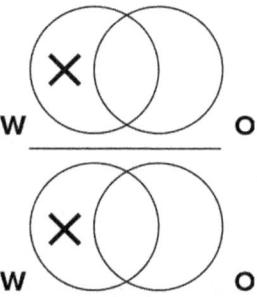

<u>It is false that some mermaids are acrobats.</u>
Some mermaids are not acrobats.

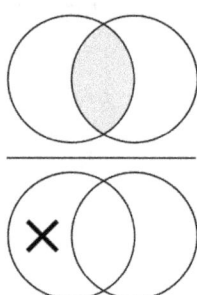

<u>Some insects are not ants.</u>
No insects are ants.

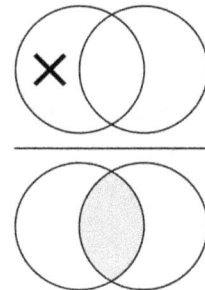

Thus far, we have applied the Boolean standpoint. However, in some cases, if the subject term denotes actually existing things, we may apply the Aristotelian interpretation so that our premises provide us with more information. Given the Aristotelian interpretation, we may be able to identify more valid arguments than if we were limited to just the Boolean standpoint. We will modify our Venn diagram method to begin with the Boolean standpoint and then follow with additional steps in order to incorporate the Aristotelian standpoint.

Consider the Aristotelian standpoint when two conditions exist:
1. The argument is invalid from the Boolean standpoint.
2. The left-hand premise circle is partially shaded.

Steps for the Aristotelian standpoint:
   I. Draw a circled X in the unshaded section of the left premise circle.
   II. Retest for validity. The three possible outcomes are as follows:
      a. The argument remains invalid.
      b. The argument is valid if the circled X really exists.
      c. The argument is invalid if the circled X does not exist.

Two of the four problems from the previous page require the Aristotelian standpoint:

All men are painters.
Some men are painters.

It is false that some mermaids are acrobats.
Some mermaids are not acrobats.

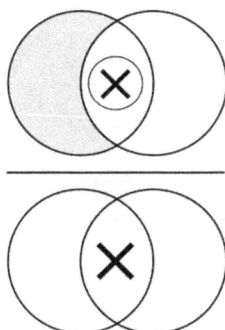
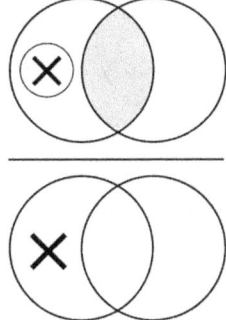

Invalid from the Boolean standpoint but valid from Aristotelian (men exist)

Invalid from the Boolean standpoint Invalid—Aristotelian (mermaids do not exist)

As we see in the previous problems, both arguments require the Aristotelian standpoint because the two conditions are met: (1) it is invalid from the Boolean standpoint, and (2) there is partial shading in the left premise circle. We then draw a circled X in the unshaded area of the left premise circle. Given this additional information in the premise, the validity of the argument may be determined. For the first argument, the circled X matches with the X in the conclusion circles. This shows that the argument is conditionally valid, and its validity will

28 | Basics of Logic

depend on the actual existence of the term. Since the terms "men" and "painters" exist, this argument is valid. With the second argument, the circled X matches with the X in the conclusion circles and so is conditionally valid. However, in this case, the term "mermaids" does not exist, so this argument is invalid.

Exercise 3-A Two-Circle Venn Diagrams

Use Venn diagrams to evaluate the following arguments. In some cases of Boolean invalidity, you may have to apply the Aristotelian standpoint. Draw Venn diagrams for the premise above the horizontal line and Venn diagrams for the conclusion below. Italicized are the terms that denote nonexisting things (e.g., unicorns, elves).

1. <u>No bikes are cars.</u>
   Some bikes are not cars.

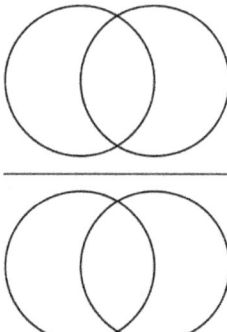

2. <u>Some rabbits are pests.</u>
   All rabbits are pests.

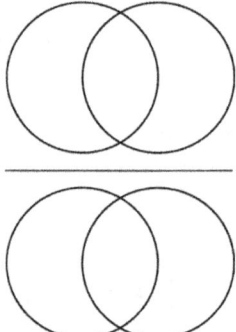

3. <u>All quarters are coins.</u>
   It is false that some quarters are not coins.

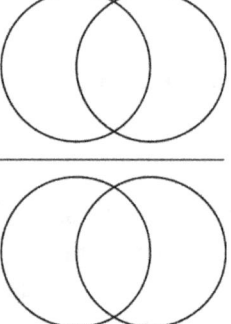

4. <u>Some pets are not frogs.</u>
   Some pets are frogs.

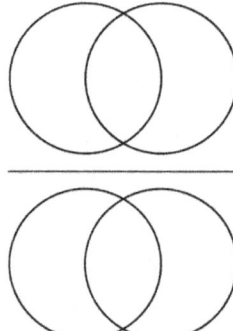

5. It is false that some goats are pets.
   No goats are pets.

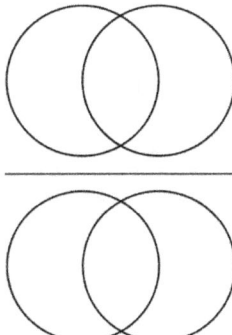

6. No cats are dogs.
   Some cats are not dogs.

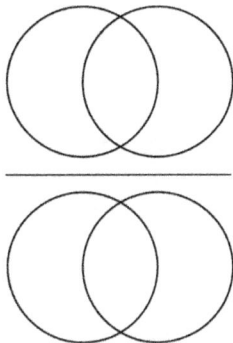

7. No scooters are trucks.
   It is false that some scooters are trucks.

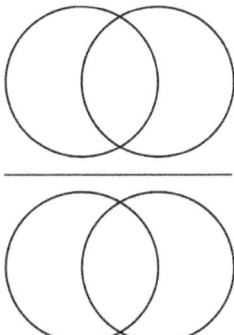

8. Some gems are not opals.
   It is false that all gems are opals.

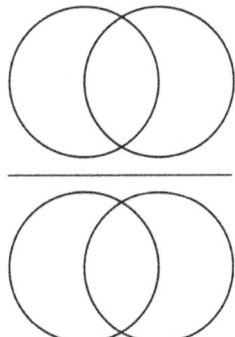

9. It is false that some *centaurs* are not humans.
   It is false that no *centaurs* are humans.

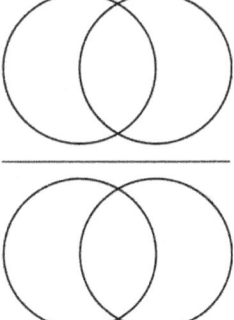

10. Some books are not dictionaries.
    No books are dictionaries.

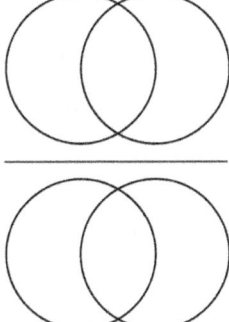

11. <u>Some women are lawyers.</u>
    Some women are not lawyers.

    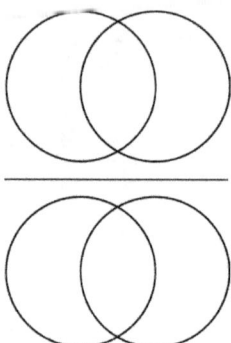

12. <u>It is false that no dimes are coins.</u>
    Some dimes are coins.

    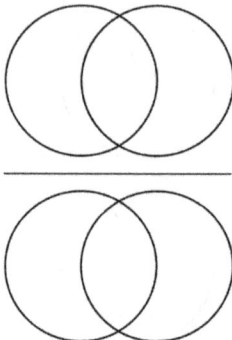

13. <u>All *ghosts* are tricksters.</u>
    Some *ghosts* are tricksters.

    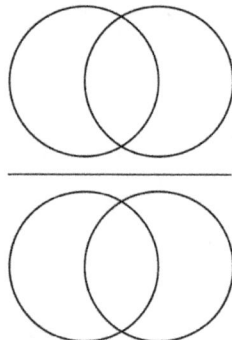

14. <u>No *unicorns* are circus animals.</u>
    Some unicorns are circus animals.

    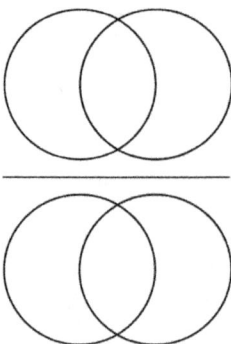

15. <u>It is false that some *mermaids* are acrobats.</u>
    No *mermaids* are acrobats.

    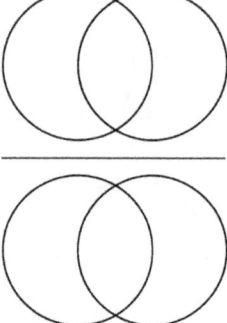

16. <u>Some insects are not ants.</u>
    It is false that all insects are ants.

    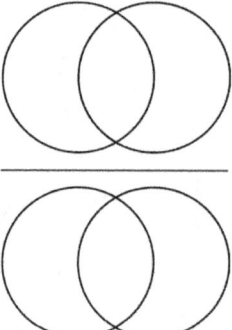

17. It is false that all men are painters.
    Some men are painters.

    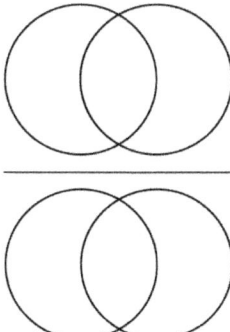

18. It is false that some *sirens* are not women.
    It is false that all *sirens* are women.

    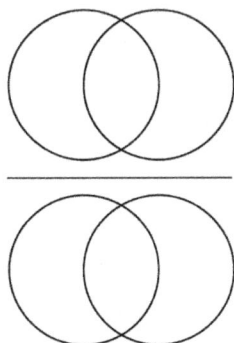

19. No *dragons* are fireflies.
    It is false that all *dragons* are fireflies.

    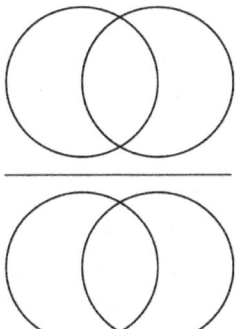

20. It is false that some forests are deserts.
    Some forests are not deserts.

    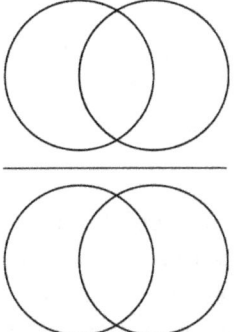

CHAPTER 4
The Square of Opposition

In Chapter 4, we will analyze other forms of categorical reasoning. We will apply the square of opposition and the relations of conversion, contraposition, and obversion to determine validity.

- Distinguish when to apply the traditional versus the modern square of opposition
- Use the square of opposition to determine the validity of immediate inferences
- Apply the relations of conversion, contraposition, and obversion to prove validity

When an immediate inference contains two corresponding categorical claims (i.e., the premise and conclusion both have the same subject term and the same predicate term), we can also determine the argument's validity by another method called the square of opposition. The **Square of Opposition** shows the logical relationships among all *corresponding* categorical claims.

We can arrange all four corresponding claims into a square of opposition:

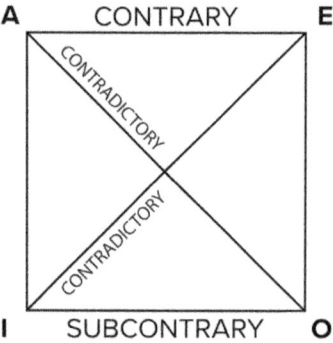

IMG 4.1 The Traditional Square of Opposition

Corresponding A- and E-claims are **contrary claims**: They are never both true. If "All rooms are vacant" is true, then "No rooms are vacant" is false. Both claims might be false. Neither "All cars are Toyotas" nor "No cars are Toyotas" is true. So, if an A- or E-claim is true, you know that its contrary is false. If an A- or E-claim is false, however, you can't draw any conclusions about its contrary. The contrary would be underdetermined, meaning that it can be true or it can be false. So, for two claims, A and E, to be contrary means that they can both be false or one may be true while the other is false, but they cannot both simultaneously be true.

> If "All patriots are conformists (A)" is true, then "No patriots are conformists (E)" must be false.
>
> If "All patriots are conformists" is false, then "No patriots are conformists (E)" is underdetermined.
>
> If "No patriots are conformists (E)" is true, then "All patriots are conformists (A)" must be false.
>
> If "No patriots are conformists (E)" is false, then "All patriots are conformists (A)" is underdetermined.

At the bottom of the square of opposition, corresponding I- and O-claims are **subcontrary claims**: They are never both false. If "Some rooms are vacant" is false, then "Some rooms are not vacant" must be true. Both might be true: "Some cars are Toyotas" and "Some cars are not Toyotas." So, if an I- or O-claim is false, you know its subcontrary is true. On the other hand, if an I-claim or an O-claim is true, you cannot draw any conclusions about its subcontrary as it may be true or false; that is, it is underdetermined. Corresponding I- and O-claims may both be true or one may be true while the other is false. The subcontrary relation requires that I- and O-claims are not both false at the same time.

> If "Some relatives are cousins (I)" is true, then "Some relatives are not cousins (O)" is undetermined.
>
> If "Some relatives are cousins (I)" is false, then "Some relatives are not cousins (O)" must be true.
>
> If "Some relatives are not cousins (O)" is true, then "Some relatives are cousins (I)" is undetermined.
>
> If "Some relatives are not cousins (O)" is false, then "Some relatives are cousins (I)" must be true.

Corresponding A- and O-claims are **contradictory claims**, as are corresponding E- and I-claims: They have opposite truth values such that if A is true, then O is false, or if A is false, then O is true. A similar contradictory relation holds between E- and I-claims.

> If "All boxers are left-handed people" is false, "Some boxers are not left-handed people" must be true.
>
> If "Some left-handed people are boxers" is true, "No left-handed people are boxers" must be false.

When you have a true A- or E-claim (at the top of the square), or a false I- or O-claim (at the bottom), you can infer the truth values of all corresponding claims. Some depictions of the traditional square also include the subalternation relation, which relates A and I as well as E and O. We will not introduce the subalternation relation here because validity may be determined by using a combination of the contrary (or subcontrary) relation with the contradictory relation.

Example 1

A – "All windows are glass objects" is true. Then:

E – "No windows are glass objects" (contrary) is false;

O – "Some windows are not glass objects" (contradictory) is false;

I – "Some windows are glass objects" (contradictory of contrary) is true.

Example 2

I – "Some cars are surfboards" is false. Then:

O – "Some cars are not surfboards" (subcontrary) is true;

E – "No cars are surfboards" (contradictory) is true;

A – "All cars are surfboards" (contradictory of the subcontrary) is false.

However, when you have a false A- or E-claim, or a true I- or O-claim, you can only infer the truth-value of its contradictory.

From the false claim "All politicians are men," all that follows is the truth of its contradictory, "Some politicians are not men."

From the true claim "Some politicians are men," all that follows is the falsity of "No politicians are men."

Whereas Aristotle devised the traditional square of opposition to include the contrary and the subcontrary relations, the logician George Boole restricted the logical relations to only the contradictory relation. Boole offers us the modern square of opposition. The modern square allows the contradictory relation between A and O, as well as between E and I. The contrary and subcontrary relations are omitted.

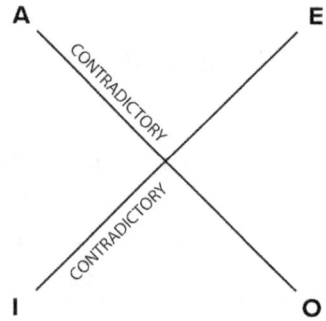

IMG 4.2 The Modern Square of Opposition

If the subject term does exist, we should apply Aristotle's traditional square, which includes the modern square plus the contrary and subcontrary relations. For example, "mermaids" and "leprechauns" do not exist. So, if we are going to apply the square of opposition to the sentences "All mermaids are swimmers" or "Some leprechauns are Irishmen," we should only apply the modern square. That is, only the contradictory relation would be applicable when the subject term does not refer to actually existing things.

Exercise 4-A Square of Opposition

These arguments are the same as those that appear in the previous chapter. Please use either the traditional or the modern square of opposition to determine whether the arguments are valid or invalid. Do your answers match the previous answers for Exercise 3-A where you used the Venn diagrams (they should)?

1. <u>No bikes are cars.</u>
   Some bikes are not cars.

2. <u>Some rabbits are pests.</u>
   All rabbits are pests.

3. <u>All quarters are coins.</u>
   It is false that some quarters are not coins.

4. <u>Some pets are not frogs.</u>
   Some pets are frogs.

5. <u>It is false that some goats are pets.</u>
   No goats are pets.

6. <u>No cats are dogs.</u>
   Some cats are not dogs.

7. <u>No scooters are trucks.</u>
   It is false that some scooters are trucks.

8. <u>Some gems are not opals.</u>
   It is false that all gems are opals.

9. <u>It is false that some centaurs are not humans.</u>
   It is false that no centaurs are humans.

10. <u>Some books are not dictionaries.</u>
    No books are dictionaries.

11. <u>Some women are lawyers.</u>
    Some women are not lawyers.

12. <u>It is false that no dimes are coins.</u>
    Some dimes are coins.

13. <u>All ghosts are tricksters.</u>
    Some ghosts are tricksters.

14. <u>No unicorns are circus animals.</u>
    Some unicorns are circus animals.

15. It is false that some mermaids are acrobats.
    No mermaids are acrobats.

16. Some insects are not ants.
    It is false that all insects are ants.

17. It is false that all men are painters.
    Some men are painters.

18. It is false that some mermaids are not women.
    It is false that all mermaids are women.

19. No *dragons* are fireflies.
    It is false that all *dragons* are fireflies.

20. It is false that some forests are deserts.
    Some forests are not deserts.

Conversion, Contraposition, and Obversion

Three operations also help us to draw simple inferences from categorical claims. To produce the **converse** of a categorical claim (a process called conversion), simply switch the subject and predicate terms. E- and I-claims are equivalent to their converses, but A- and O-claims are not. When we say, "No cats are dogs," it is equivalent to saying, "No dogs are cats." Similarly, the claim "Some doctors are men" is equivalent to the sentence, "Some men are doctors." An immediate inference starting with a categorical claim and concluding its converse is a valid argument when conversion is applied to an E- or I-claim. As a way to remember this, we can simply identify the second and third vowels of the word "conversion."

CONVERSION: (1) Switch subject and predicate terms.

Valid argument or equivalent statements result for E and I.

To produce the **obverse** of a standard-form claim (a process called obversion), there are two requirements. First, we must change the quality of the categorical claim, converting it from affirmative to negative, or vice versa. Second, we must replace the predicate term with its **complementary term**. A term's complement names every member of the universe of discourse that is not included in the class of things denoted by the term. Usually, the complementary term can be formed with the prefix "non" in front of the original term: "democracy" and "non-democracy." Sometimes we need to take care to restrict the universe of discourse. The term complementary to "drivers" is "people who are not drivers." Strictly speaking, the complement to "people who are happy" is not "people who are sad" but "people who are not happy."

OBVERSION: (1) Change the quality (affirmative to negative, or vice versa) and (2) take the complement of the predicate term.

Valid argument or equivalent statements result for E and I.

Changing a claim from affirmative to negative, or vice versa, is the same as going horizontally across the square of opposition. An A-claim changes to an E-claim, or the other way around, by exchanging the quantifier "all" to "no" or vice versa. An I-claim changes to an O-claim, or an O-claim changes to an I-claim by way of the copula being "are" or "are not." All claims are equivalent to their obverses. "All blessings are mixed things" becomes, through obversion, "No blessings are unmixed things." Similarly, saying, "Some athletes are pros" amounts to saying, "Some athletes are not nonpros." It does not matter what claims we are dealing with, whether we start off or end up with an A, E, I, or O claim because an obversion will always lead to equivalent statements. A categorical claim and its obverse would make for a valid argument if one of the statements is the premise and the other is the conclusion of an immediate inference.

To produce the **contrapositive** of a claim (a process known as contraposition), there are also two requirements. The first is the same as the condition for conversion: switch the subject and predicate terms. The second requirement is to replace both the subject and the predicate terms with their complementary terms. A- and O-claims are equivalent to their contrapositives, but E- and I-claims are not. Moreover, claims that are not equivalent to their converses are equivalent to their contrapositives. "All poodles are dogs" is equivalent to "All nondogs are nonpoodles." "Some employees are not guards" is equivalent to "Some nonguards are not nonemployees." Just as with the word "conversion," the second and third vowels of the word "contraposition" reveals the categorical claims that yield equivalent contrapositives – A and O.

> CONTRAPOSITION: (1) Switch subject and predicate terms and (2) take the complement of both subject and predicate terms.
>
> Valid argument or equivalent statements result for A and O.

Example 1:	**Some old dogs are loyal pets.**	**I-claim**
Conversion	Some loyal pets are old dogs.	Equivalent
Contraposition	Some disloyal pets are young dogs.	Not Equivalent
Obversion	Some old dogs are not disloyal pets.	Equivalent

Example 2:	**All humans are mortal beings.**	**A-claim**
Conversion	All mortal beings are humans.	Not Equivalent
Contraposition	All immortal beings are nonhumans.	Equivalent
Obversion	No humans are immortal beings.	Equivalent

38 | Basics of Logic

Exercise 4-B Conversion Contraposition Obversion

Write out the resulting statement. Is the new statement equivalent to the original one?

1. What is the contrapositive of "All chemistry experiments are science experiments"?
2. What is the converse of "Some psychology majors are not Freud fans"?
3. What is the obverse of "Some athletes are persons who cannot run marathons"?
4. What is the contrapositive of "Some tall people are ungraceful dancers"?
5. What is the obverse of "All caused actions are nonfree acts"?
6. What is the converse of "All philosophy majors are Plato fans"?
7. What is the contrapositive of "No old dogs are pets who can learn new tricks"?
8. What is the converse of "No unhappy events are good memories"?
9. What is the obverse of "Some science majors are tidy individuals"?
10. What is the contrapositive of "Some law-abiding citizens are not moral people"?
11. What is the obverse of "No healthy snacks are tasty treats"?
12. What is the obverse of "Some lost items are things people treasure"?

Exercise 4-C Determine Validity

Apply conversion, obversion, or contraposition to determine whether the following arguments are valid or invalid.

1. Some living things are mortal creatures.
   Some immortal creatures are nonliving things.

2. All unforgettable memories are meaningful recollections.
   No unforgettable memories are unmeaningful recollections.

3. No striped zebras are spotted leopards.
   No spotted leopards are striped zebras.

4. Some unpicked cherries are not ripe berries.
   Some unripe berries are not picked cherries.

5. Some unfriendly guests are unkind people.
   Some unfriendly guests are not kind people.

6. No uneducated buffoons are people who read constantly.
   No people who read constantly are educated buffoons.

7. All responsible students are disciplined persons.
   All disciplined persons are responsible students.

8. Some forbidden desires are unhealthy cravings.
   Some healthy cravings are unforbidden desires.

9. No trained performers are wild animals.
   All trained performers are domesticated animals.

10. Some exciting activities are not planned events.
    Some exciting activities are unplanned events.

11. No men who can bake are uncreative cooks.
    No creative cooks are men who cannot bake.

12. All imaginary friends are childhood fantasies.
    All childhood fantasies are imaginary friends.

Exercise 4-D Combining Methods

Use either the square of opposition or conversion, obversion, or contraposition to determine whether the following arguments are valid or invalid. Explain your answer. Remember that the square applies to arguments with corresponding statements (same subject and predicate terms in the premise and in the conclusion).

1. It is false that some tooth fairies are daytime visitors. Therefore, some tooth fairies are not daytime visitors.
2. No broken vases are indestructible containers. Therefore, no containers that can be destroyed are unbroken vases.
3. All porcelain figurines are fragile artifacts. Therefore, no porcelain figurines are nonfragile artifacts.
4. It is false that some psychoanalysts are not individuals driven by religious fervor. So, it is false that some psychoanalysts are individuals driven by religious fervor.
5. Some biology majors are lazy students. Therefore, some industrious students are non-biology majors.
6. No flying unicorns are animals who get lost in the fog. So, it is false that all flying unicorns are animals who get lost in the fog.
7. Some economists are not followers of Ayn Rand. Therefore, some followers of Ayn Rand are not economists.
8. Some pleasant recollections are not missed opportunities. Therefore, some availed opportunities are not unpleasant recollections.
9. It is false that some human beings are lawyers. So, some human beings are not lawyers.
10. Some students are undeclared majors. So, some students are not declared majors.
11. No despicable persons are moral paragons. Thus, some despicable persons are not moral paragons.
12. All citizens are residents. Therefore, no citizens are nonresidents.
13. Some kangaroos are marsupials. Therefore, it is false that some kangaroos are not marsupials.

14. No leprechauns are generous creatures. Therefore, it is false that all leprechauns are generous creatures.
15. Some sharks are carnivores. So, some carnivores are sharks.
16. Some liberals are losers. So, some winners are conservatives.
17. Some people are entrepreneurs. So, all people are entrepreneurs.
18. Some effects are not expected outcomes. Therefore, some effects are unexpected outcomes.
19. All current viewers are mature persons. Hence, it is false that no current viewers are mature persons.
20. No loud noises are pleasant sounds. Consequently, no pleasant sounds are loud noises.

CHAPTER 5
Translation into Standard-Form Categorical

> In Chapter 5, we will convert ordinary English sentences into categorical claims in standard form. We will also define categorical syllogisms in standard form and apply the charts method to determine the validity of such arguments.
> - Convert English sentences into categorical claims in standard form
> - Recognize whether a categorical syllogism is in standard form
> - Identify the mood and figure of a categorical syllogism
> - Apply the charts method to determine the validity of categorical syllogisms

There are four standard-form categorical claims, having the letter name: A, E, I, or O. To be in standard form, a categorical claim must begin with the word "all," "no," or "some." The first word of a categorical claim is known as the "quantifier," which indicates how much of the subject term we are discussing. Also, the verb or the copula must be "are" and sometimes "are not" for O-claims. Finally, the terms in standard-form categorical claims must be plural nouns. For example, because it contains singular nouns and does not begin with a quantifier, the claim "A ruby is a gem" is not in standard form but the equivalent categorical claim "All rubies are gems" is in standard form. Likewise, the claims "Some metals are golden" and "No coins are in the cash register" are not in standard form because not all the terms are plural nouns.

A surprising number of ordinary sentences can be converted into categorical claims in standard form. Many ordinary claims need only small changes before taking on the standard form of A-, E-, I-, or O-claims. Claims about whole classes require only the addition or substitution of words like "all" and "no." "Each student is a responsible adult" thus turns into "All students are responsible adults." "Students are not idle people" may be converted to a standard-form E-claim: "No students are idle people."

Conditional statements may be converted to either A- or E-claims. Conditionals of the form **"If A, then B"** are translated into A-claims that may read "All things [people, times, places, and so on] that are A are things that are B. Similarly, conditional statements that express a negative message such as **"If A, then not B"** could be expressed as E-claims—namely, "No things that are A are things that are B." For example, the sentences "If it is a raccoon, then it will steal the food" and "If it is a slow car, then it is not a racecar" may be translated "All raccoons are animals that will steal food" and "No slow cars are racecars," respectively. Sometimes the word "if" may appear in the middle of the conditional statement. The sentence "It will steal food if it is a raccoon" may be expressed as the same A-claim "All raccoons are animals that will steal food." Thus, moving the word "if" from the front to the middle of the conditional statement makes no difference. However, with the phrase **"only if,"** the words that follow "only if" go in the predicate term position (i.e., toward the end of the sentence). "Students pass only if they studied" is translated to "All students who pass are students who studied."

Keep in mind that when you translate an ordinary English sentence into a categorical claim in standard form, you must stick to the proper form:

1. Claims must begin with the words "all," "no," or "some."
2. The verb must be "are" and only with O-claims the verb may be "are not."
3. The terms must be plural nouns (not adjectives and not singular nouns).

The phrases "not every" and "not all" may begin a sentence. This sentence may be thought of as the negation of an A-claim. By the square of opposition, if A is false, then its contradictory O would have to be true. Thus, "Not every/all A are B" is equivalent to an O-claim of the form "Some A are not B." Similarly, a sentence may read "Not a single A is B." This is equivalent to saying, "It is not the case that some A are B," which is the negation of an I-statement. By the square of opposition, if I is false, then its contradictory E must be true. So, "Not a single A is B" may be converted to an E-claim, "No A are B."

The following is a list of ordinary sentences along with their standard-form categorical claim equivalent:

A tiger has stripes.	*All tigers are animals that have stripes.*
A few officers are promoted.	*Some officers are promoted persons.*
There are muffins in the oven.	*Some muffins are items in the oven.*
A tomato is not a vegetable.	*No tomatoes are vegetables.*
Soldiers are not cowards.	*No soldiers are cowards.*
He is a father only if he is male.	*All fathers are males.*
Not a single voter is left-handed.	*No voters are left-handed persons.*
Not all dancers sing well.	*Some dancers are not good singers.*
Anything that breathes lives.	*All things that breathe are things that live.*
Anyone who stays is brave.	*All people who stay are brave people.*
If she is a violinist, she's a musician.	*All violinists are musicians.*
If he's a child, then he's not an adult.	*No children are adults.*
She is a citizen if she can vote.	*All voters are citizens.*
Nothing is a round square.	*No things are round squares.*
It is an odd number if it is not even.	*No even numbers are odd numbers.*

Exercise 5-A Categorical Translations

Convert these sentences into standard-form categorical claims.

1. There are days in the week that are not holidays.
2. Every koala is a marsupial.
3. If it is a dog, then it is a smart animal.
4. If it is a cat, then it is an animal that is not going to cooperate.
5. It's a kangaroo only if it is a marsupial.
6. An animal cannot learn new tricks if it's an old dog.
7. Anything that's a snake is a reptile.
8. All villains oppose law and order.
9. Professors are educators.
10. A horse is an animal.
11. It's a US coin if it's a bicentennial quarter.
12. Anything that's a rabbit is a mammal.
13. Not every friendly dog is a well-trained animal.
14. There are people who support change.
15. A few holidays fall on Sundays.
16. Someone drives a pink Cadillac.
17. There are jobs that are not safe occupations.
18. Anyone who is a painter is an artist.
19. Not a single voter supports terrorism.
20. If it's a pentagon, then it is not a parallelogram.
21. They are members only if they are conservatives.
22. Nothing is free.
23. Someone is a fast worker.
24. It's a square only if it's a rectangle.
25. Not a single cowboy can run the rodeo.
26. If it is a beach day, then it is not a rainy day.
27. If he's Bavarian, then he can yodel.
28. Not all criminals are thieves.
29. A crocodile is not an amphibian.
30. It is poisonous if it is a rattlesnake.
31. No one is a kind terrorist.
32. Not every politician is corrupt.
33. A dictionary is a reference book.
34. The day is cold if it is not sunny.
35. Only if it is a moral action, it is a permissible act.

Categorical Syllogisms in Standard Form

To make obvious the similarities of structure shared by different syllogisms, we will always present each of them in the same way (i.e., in standard form). Just as a categorical claim may be in standard form, a categorical syllogism may be expressed in standard form. When we have a standard-form categorical syllogism, we may apply several methods to it to determine its validity. A **categorical syllogism in standard form** is always an argument consisting of exactly three categorical claims (two premises and a conclusion). Additionally, in a standard-form categorical syllogism, there are also three categorical terms, each of which is used exactly twice. One of these terms does not occur in the conclusion but does appear once in each of the premises. This special term is called the **middle term**.

Consider the following example of a categorical syllogism in standard form.
No geese are felines.
<u>Some birds are geese.</u>
Therefore, some birds are not felines.

The last sentence, "Some birds are not felines," is the conclusion of this syllogism. Each term (geese, felines, and birds) is repeated twice. "Geese" is the **middle term** of the syllogism. There are also two other terms called the major term and the minor term. The major term appears in the first premise, traditionally called the major premise; the major term also occurs as the predicate term of the conclusion. The minor term appears somewhere in the second premise, called the minor premise. The minor term is also the subject term of the conclusion. In the previous example, the major term is "felines," and the minor term is "birds."

The stipulation for the location of the major and minor terms is another condition for a categorical syllogism to be in standard form. We can call this the reverse-order rule. Note the term "felines" appears in the first premise, and the term "birds" appears in the second premise. The position of these two terms is reversed in the conclusion, where "birds" appears first in the conclusion (subject term), while "felines" appears second (predicate term).

Conditions for standard-form categorical claims:

1. There are two premises and one conclusion with each statement being an A, E, I, or O standard-form claim.
2. There are exactly three terms, each term being a plural noun and appearing twice in the argument.
3. The location of the terms:
    a. The middle term appears once in each premise.
    b. Reverse-Order Rule: The other two terms appear in Premise 1 or 2. If term X appears in Premise 1 and Y appears in Premise 2, then X would be the predicate term (second position), and Y would be the subject term (first position) of the conclusion.

Only one of the following arguments is a categorical syllogism in standard form. Can you identify it and explain why the others are not in standard form?

Example One
Some flowers are not daisies.
No oaks are daisies.
No flower is an oak.

Example Two
Some flowers are roses.
Some flowers are lilies.
No lilies are roses.

Example Three
All roses are flowers.
No roses are elms.
All elms are not roses.

Example Four
Some roses are red.
No violets are roses.
No violets are red.

Because it meets all the conditions, Example Two is a categorical syllogism in standard form. All three statements are categorical claims in standard form, and there are three plural terms that appear twice in the argument. Example Two also meets the reverse-order rule. For, the terms in the conclusion appear in this order: first "lilies" as the subject term and second "roses" as the predicate term. These terms appear in reverse order in the premises with "roses" in the first premise and "lilies" in the second premise.

There are several problems in the other examples that keep them from being in standard form. For Example One, the conclusion is not in standard form since an E-claim should have "are" as its copula and the terms should be plural. Also, Example One does not follow the reverse-order rule since the conclusion terms appear in the order of "flowers" followed by "oaks." Yet, "flowers" is contained in the first premise, and "oaks" is in the second premise. Two problems also keep Example Three from being in standard form. The term "roses" appears three times, while "flowers" appears only once. Each of the three terms in a categorical syllogism should appear exactly twice in different sentences. The second problem with Example Three lies with the conclusion, which is not an A-claim since its copula is "are not." Example Four is not in standard form because "red" is not an appropriate term. All terms in a categorical syllogism should be plural nouns. This can be corrected if we change the word "red" to "red things."

Exercise 5-B Categorical Syllogisms

Determine if the following arguments are categorical syllogisms in standard form. If the argument is not in standard form, make some changes to turn it into a categorical syllogism in standard form. You may need to convert a sentence into a standard-form categorical statement (A, E, I O), change the order of the premises, or turn singular terms into plural form.

1. Some farmers hunt wild game.
   There are farmers who are cattle ranchers.
   Some cattle ranchers are hunters of wild game.

2. If it is a horse, then it is a mammal.
   <u>If it is a stallion, then it is a horse.</u>
   If it is a stallion, then it is a mammal.

3. They are supporters only if they are libertarians.
   <u>Some supporters are economists.</u>
   Some economists are libertarians.

4. Not all short-haired cats are stray animals.
   <u>No hospital's residents are stray animals.</u>
   Some hospital residents are not short-haired cats.

5. Some open windows are not locked doors.
   <u>Some locked doors are not wide apertures.</u>
   No wide apertures are open windows.

6. Some blood donors are not extravagant misers.
   <u>No person is an extravagant miser.</u>
   Some persons are blood donors.

7. A captain is a military officer.
   <u>No private is a military officer.</u>
   No privates are captains.

8. Some oaks are not elms.
   <u>It is an elm only if it is a tree.</u>
   Some trees are oaks.

9. Some instructors are math teachers.
   <u>If they are math teachers, then they are persons.</u>
   Not every person is an instructor.

10. All accidents are unfortunate occurrences.
    <u>Some accidents are blessings in disguise.</u>
    No unfortunate occurrences are blessings in disguise.

11. Not a single war hero is a coward.
    <u>Some cowards own loaded pistols.</u>
    Some owners of loaded pistols are heroes.

12. No pink parasols are brown trousers.
    <u>Some hair ornaments are not pink parasols.</u>
    No hair ornaments are brown trousers.

The Charts Method

One method for evaluating categorical syllogism in standard form is the **Charts Method**, which involves identifying the mood and figure of a syllogism. Medieval logicians devised a simple way of labeling the various forms in which a categorical syllogism may occur by stating its mood and figure. The **mood** of a syllogism identifies the categorical statements (**A**, **E**, **I**, or **O**) in the argument, listed in the order in which they appear in the standard-form categorical syllogism. Thus, a syllogism with a mood of **OAO** has an **O** proposition as its first premise, an **A** proposition as its second premise, and another **O** proposition as its conclusion; an **EIO** syllogism has an **E** premise, and **I** premise, and an **O** conclusion, in that order.

The **figure** of a categorical syllogism is determined by the position in which its middle term appears in the two premises: in a first-figure syllogism, the middle term is the subject term of the first premise and the predicate term of the second premise; in a second figure, the middle term is the predicate term of both premises; in a third figure, the middle term is the subject term of both premises; and in a fourth figure, the middle term appears as the predicate term of the first premise and the subject term of the second premise. The four figures are illustrated in this simple chart showing the position of the terms as they would appear in the premises (M is the middle term, S is the subject term of the conclusion, and P is the predicate term of the conclusion):

Figure 1:	M	P
	S	M
Figure 2:	P	M
	S	M
Figure 3:	M	P
	M	S
Figure 4:	P	M
	M	S

All told, there are exactly 256 distinct forms of a categorical syllogism. Used together, the mood and figure provide a way of describing the unique logical structure of each categorical syllogism. The following are two examples of categorical syllogisms and their moods and figures.

Example One IAI-3
Some merchants are pirates.
All merchants are swimmers.
Some swimmers are pirates.

Example Two AEE-4
All sapphires are gems.
No gems are rhinestones.
No rhinestones are sapphires.

Both of these categorical syllogisms are valid. An argument is valid just in case the conclusion must be true if we assume that the premises are true. That is, the conclusion may be said to follow necessarily from the premises.

We can also prove the validity of categorical syllogisms by looking them up on two special charts devised by Aristotle. The easier of these two charts is the unconditionally valid chart, which lists 15 valid forms. The two examples may be found on this unconditionally valid chart. The mood IAI is listed under the Figure 3 column and AEE is listed under the Figure 4 column. It is important to locate the mood under the exact figure. For example, IAI-2 would be invalid because we do not find IAI under Figure 2, although IAI appears under Figures 3 and 4. If an argument is **unconditionally valid**, then it is valid no matter what, and there are no additional requirements.

TABLE 5.1 Unconditionally Valid Forms

Figure:	1	2	3	4
Mood:	AAA	EAE	IAI	AEE
	EAE	AEE	AII	IAI
	AII	EIO	OAO	EIO
	EIO	AOO	EIO	

Unlike the unconditionally valid chart, the conditionally valid chart imposes additional requirements on the syllogism. If the mood and figure of a particular categorical syllogism are found on the conditionally valid chart, then it is conditionally valid, which means it is valid if a certain condition is satisfied.

TABLE 5.2 Conditionally Valid Forms

Figure:	1	2	3	4	Condition
Mood:	AAI	AEO		AEO	if S exists
	EAO	EAO			
			AAI	EAO	if M exists
			EAO		
				AAI	if P exists

The condition is specified on the rightmost column of the chart under the heading "Condition." The conditions are abbreviated: **S** stands for the **subject term of the conclusion**, **M** for **middle term**, and **P** for the **predicate term of the conclusion**. For a categorical syllogism that is conditionally valid, we must look across the row in which the mood/figure is listed and consider the specified condition. If the condition is "S exists," then we must identify the subject term of the conclusion and determine whether this term denotes actually existing things. If S does actually exist, then the syllogism is valid; otherwise, it is invalid.

Example One AAI-4

All gems are diamonds.
All diamonds are stones.
Some stones are gems.
Valid if P (gems) exist.
So, answer is valid.

Example Two EAO-4

No fairies are mermaids.
All mermaids are rational creatures.
Some rational creatures are not fairies.
Valid if M (mermaids) exist.
So, answer is invalid.

Example Three AEO-2

All elixirs are magic potions.
No sodas are magic potions.
Some sodas are not elixirs.
Valid if S (sodas) exist.
So, answer is valid.

Example Four AEO-3

All goblins are monsters.
No goblins are dragons.
Some dragons are not monsters.
Not on conditionally valid chart and
Not on unconditionally valid chart.
So, argument is invalid.

Exercise 5-C The Charts Method

Determine validity by the charts method.

1. All marsupials are animals.
   All koalas are marsupials.
   All koalas are animals.

2. Some cities are state capitals.
   All state capitals are familiar places.
   Some familiar places are cities.

3. Some dictionaries are books.
   Some paper goods are books.
   Some paper goods are dictionaries.

4. All dictionaries are books.
   No dictionaries are comics.
   All comics are books.

5. All stallions are horses.
   Some pets are not horses.
   Some pets are not stallions.

6. Some lawyers are not politicians.
   All senators are politicians.
   Some senators are not lawyers.

7. Some warriors are not men.
   All actors are men.
   All actors are warriors.

8. Some gems are diamonds.
   All diamonds are stones.
   Some stones are gems.

9. No cherries are apples.
    Some strawberries are not apples.
    No strawberries are cherries.

10. No werewolves are athletes.
    All werewolves are professionals.
    Some professionals are not athletes.

11. Some furniture are tables.
    Some tables are not desks.
    All desks are furniture.

12. No humans are genies.
    All genies are rational creatures.
    Some rational creatures are not human.

13. All leprechauns are millionaires.
    No paupers are millionaires.
    Some paupers are not leprechauns.

14. All pixies are sprites.
    No bees are sprites.
    Some bees are not pixies.

15. Some ballerinas are not wrestlers.
    All ballerinas are dancers.
    Some dancers are not wrestlers.

16. No free acts are caused actions.
    All human acts are caused actions.
    So, no human acts are free acts.

17. All gymnasts are athletes.
    Some dancers are gymnasts.
    Some dancers are athletes.

18. All geniuses are smart persons.
    All wizards are geniuses.
    Some wizards are smart persons.

19. Some shoes are boots.
    Some gloves are not shoes.
    No gloves are boots.

20. All bats are winged creatures.
    All winged creatures are fairies.
    Some fairies are bats.

21. All vampires are carnivores.
    All vampires are garlic haters.
    Some garlic haters are carnivores.

22. All dogs are canines.
    No canines are felines.
    No felines are dogs.

23. All pixies are sprites.
    No sprites are hummingbirds.
    Some hummingbirds are not pixies.

24. No optimists are skeptics.
    All leprechauns are optimists.
    Some leprechauns are not skeptics.

CHAPTER 6
Three-Circle Venn Diagrams

> In Chapter 6, we will employ more methods for evaluating the validity of categorical syllogisms.
> - Represent standard-form categorical syllogisms in three-circle Venn diagrams
> - Distinguish the Aristotelian versus the Boolean ways of interpreting categorical syllogisms
> - Determine the validity of categorical syllogisms using Venn diagrams
> - Apply the four rules for determining the validity of categorical syllogisms

Recall the four **standard-form categorical claims** and their letter names:

A: All _____ are _____.

E: No _____ are _____.

I: Some _____ are _____.

O: Some _____ are not _____.

Through two-circle Venn diagrams, we have given a visual representation of each of the four categorical claims. Since there were only two terms in each categorical claim, two circles sufficed, the left-hand circle for the subject term and the right-hand circle for the predicate term. For A- and E-claims, we shaded a certain section that expressed that the section had no members; the shaded section was an empty set. On the other hand, we marked an X in the circles to express I- and O-claims which have existential import. An X in a given section of a Venn diagram states that there exists at least one thing in that area; the section is not empty.

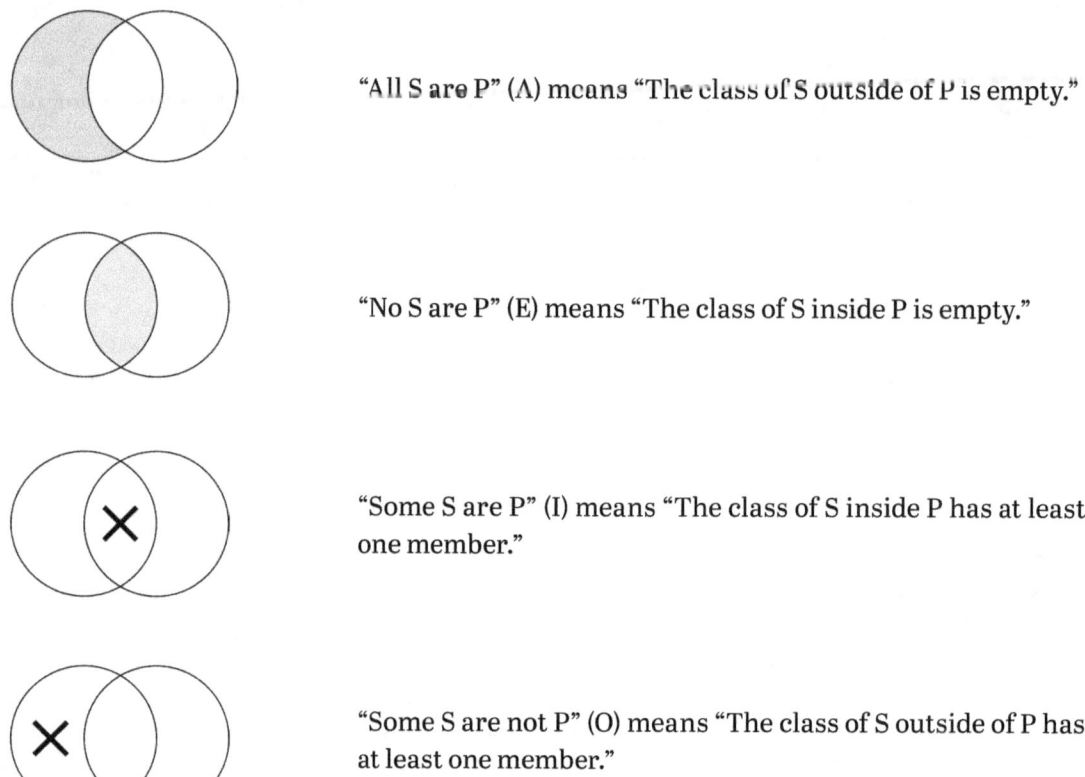

"All S are P" (A) means "The class of S outside of P is empty."

"No S are P" (E) means "The class of S inside P is empty."

"Some S are P" (I) means "The class of S inside P has at least one member."

"Some S are not P" (O) means "The class of S outside of P has at least one member."

The Three-Circle Venn Diagram Method

We now will move from two circles to three circles for Venn diagrams applied to categorical syllogisms. Immediate inferences contained only one categorical claim as its only premise, but for categorical syllogisms, there are two premises and there are three terms, repeated twice, in the argument. These three terms must appear in specific places in the categorical syllogism. Let us reconsider this example of a categorical syllogism:

No geese are felines.

Some birds are geese.

Therefore, some birds are not felines.

The three terms in this categorical syllogism include geese, felines, and birds. One of these terms, the middle term, is the term that appears once in each premise (i.e., geese).

One method for determining the validity of categorical syllogisms is the charts method in which we identify the mood and figure and consult the unconditionally valid and conditionally valid charts. Another method for determining the validity of categorical syllogisms is the **Venn Diagram** method. Just as we did for two-circle Venn diagrams, we will first construct three-circle Venn diagrams that implement only the **Boolean** interpretation. Let us consider two examples that consist of only universal categorical propositions (only A and E statements).

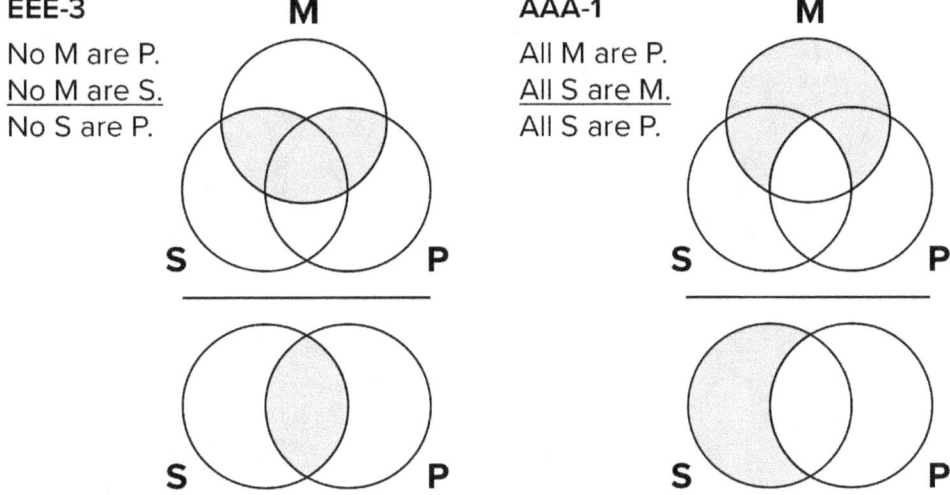

Steps for Drawing Universal Premises in Venn Diagrams (Boolean)

1. First, draw three overlapping circles and label them. Label the top middle circle above the horizontal line as the middle term (the term that appears once in each premise). Label the bottom two circles above and below the horizontal line as the subject term and predicate term of the conclusion.
2. Draw the premises above the horizontal line and the conclusion below the line. For each premise, consider only two circles at a time, ignoring the third circle.
3. Compare the premise diagrams with the conclusion diagram.
4. Determine validity by asking whether the conclusion necessarily follows from the premises. That is, does the conclusion have to be true given the premise diagrams? If yes, then the syllogism is valid. If not, then the syllogism is invalid (from the Boolean standpoint).

The next set of examples is slightly more complex because they will contain particular premises (i.e., premises that require drawing an "X"). We will need to introduce additional guidelines for drawing X's in Venn diagrams:

Steps for Drawing "X's" in Venn Diagrams

I. Always draw a universal premise before a particular premise.
II. Draw X's in your premise circles either
    a. on the dividing line between two unshaded sections, or
    b. on the unshaded section (when the other side is already shaded).

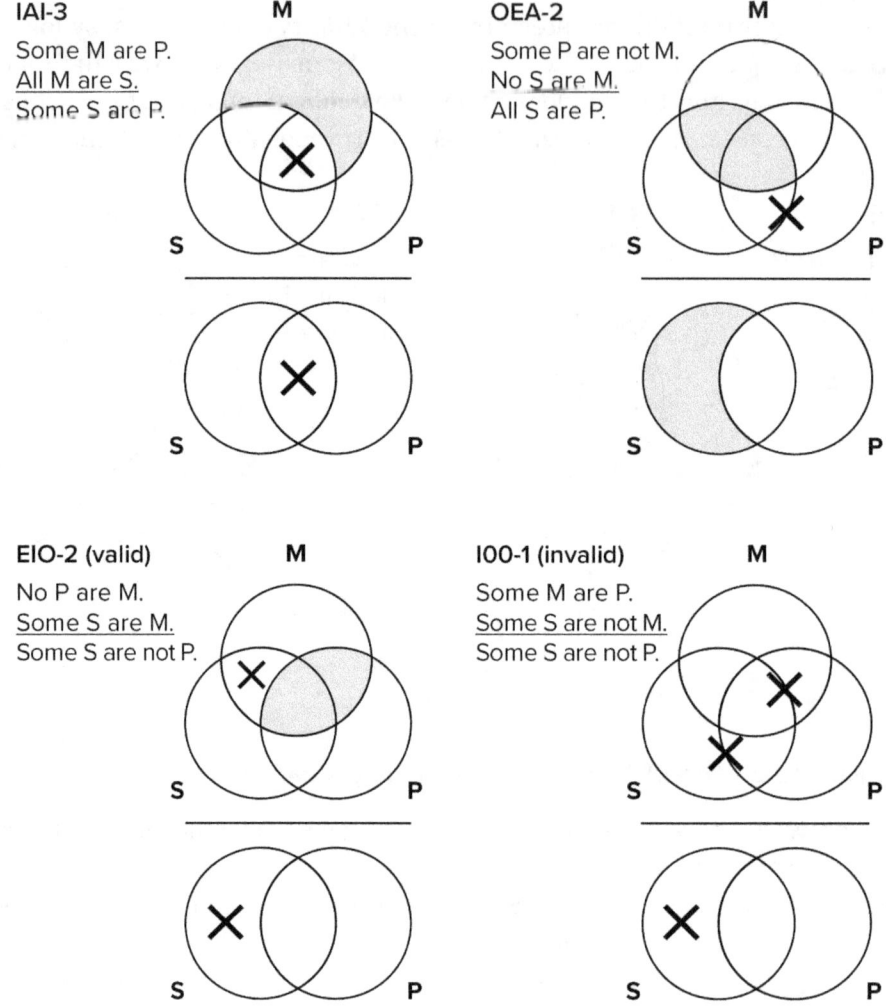

To determine the validity of some categorical syllogisms, the **Boolean** standpoint may not be sufficient. Some arguments require the application of **the Aristotelian standpoint**. Aristotle, unlike Boole, had assumed that universal statements A and E have existential import. After applying the Aristotelian standpoint, we will find that some arguments that were invalid under the Boolean standpoint are valid under the Aristotelian standpoint. When the Aristotelian standpoint applies, the argument may be conditionally valid with validity depending on the existence of a certain term.

When to apply the Aristotelian standpoint? When these two conditions occur:

1. The argument is invalid from the Boolean standpoint.
2. There is a premise circle that is shaded in all sections except for one (i.e., three out of four sections).

CHAPTER 6 Three-Circle Venn Diagrams | 55

Steps for the Aristotelian standpoint (three circles)

I. Draw a circled X in that one unshaded section of the almost completely shaded premise circle.
II. Retest for validity.
   a. The argument remains invalid.
   b. The argument is now conditionally valid: valid if a certain term exists. This term corresponds to the circle that is almost completely shaded.

AAI-4
All gems are diamonds.
All diamonds are stones.
Some stones are gems.

Answer
Boolean: Invalid
Aristotlean: Valid, since gems exist

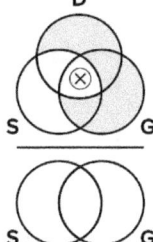

EAI-4
No fireflies are dragonflies.
All dragonflies are insects.
Some insects are fireflies.

Answer
Boolean: Invalid
Aristotlean: Invalid

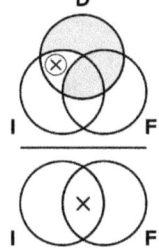

AEO-2
Some pilsners are magic potions.
No sodas are magic potions.
Some sodas are not pilsners.

Answer
Boolean: Invalid
Aristotlean: Valid, since sodas exist

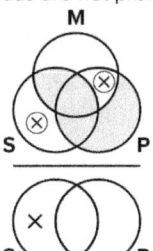

AEO-3
All gladiators are fighters.
No gladiators are pacifists.
Some pacifists are not fighters.

Answer
Boolean: Invalid
Aristotlean: Invalid

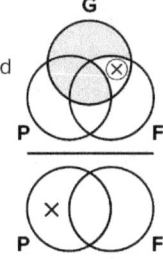

AAO-1
All gorillas are primates.
All silverbacks are gorillas.
Some silverbacks are not primates.

Answer
Boolean: Invalid
Aristotlean: Invalid

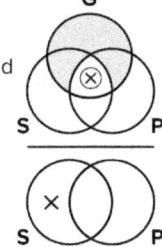

EAO-4
No dragons are rabbits.
All rabbits are mammals.
Some mammals are not dragons.

Answer
Boolean: Invalid
Aristotlean: Valid, since rabbits exist.

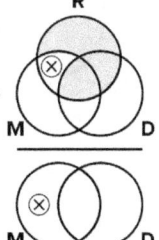

Exercise 6-A Three-Circle Venn Diagram Method

Apply the Venn diagram method to the categorical syllogisms in the following pages. These categorical syllogisms are already in standard form. Which arguments require only the Boolean standpoint? Which arguments require the Aristotelian standpoint? Apply the Aristotelian standpoints to the arguments that require it. Then determine whether the argument is valid or invalid.

1. All marsupials are animals.
   <u>All koalas are marsupials.</u>
   All koalas are animals.

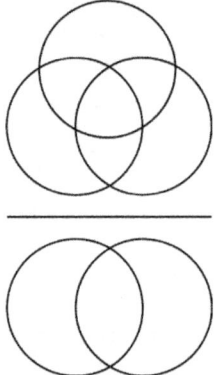

2. Some cities are state capitals.
   <u>All state capitals are familiar places.</u>
   Some familiar places are cities.

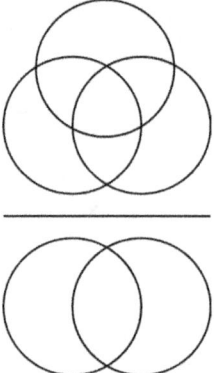

3. All dictionaries are books.
   <u>No dictionaries are comics.</u>
   All comics are books.

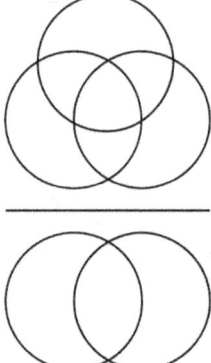

4. Some dictionaries are books.
   <u>Some paper goods are books.</u>
   Some paper goods are dictionaries.

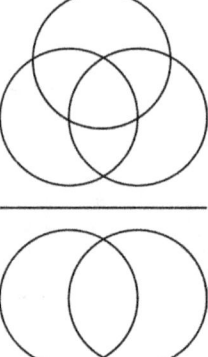

17. All gymnasts are athletes.
    <u>Some dancers are gymnasts.</u>
    Some dancers are athletes.

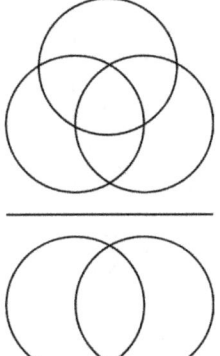

18. All geniuses are smart persons.
    <u>All wizards are geniuses.</u>
    Some wizards are smart persons.

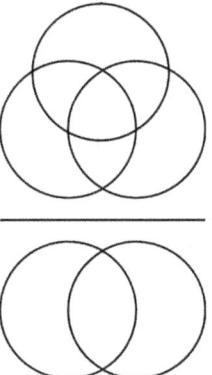

19. Some shoes are boots.
    <u>Some gloves are not shoes.</u>
    No gloves are boots.

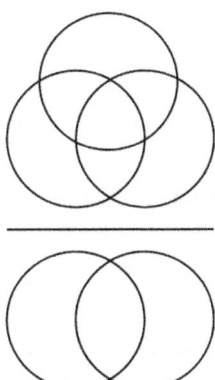

20. All bats are winged creatures.
    <u>All winged creatures are fairies.</u>
    Some fairies are bats.

21. All vampires are carnivores.
    <u>All vampires are garlic haters.</u>
    Some garlic haters are carnivores.

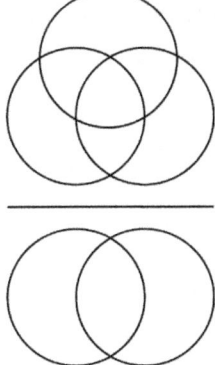

22. All dogs are canines.
    <u>No canines are felines.</u>
    No felines are dogs.

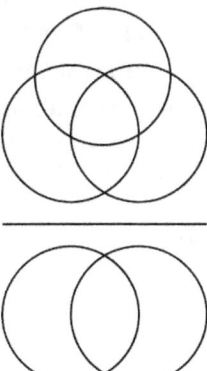

23. All pixies are sprites.
    <u>No sprites are hummingbirds.</u>
    Some hummingbirds are not pixies.

24. No optimists are skeptics.
    <u>All leprechauns are optimists.</u>
    Some leprechauns are not skeptics.

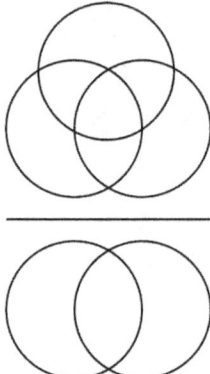

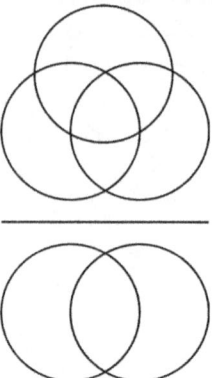

The Four Rules Method

A set of **Four Rules** provides a third method for testing a categorical syllogism's validity. To use the rules, we first need to feel comfortable with the distinction between affirmative and negative claims. A- and I-claims are affirmative; E- and O-claims are negative. Negative claims begin with the word "no" or contain the word "not."

Second, we need to introduce the concept of **distributed terms**. A term is a distributed term if the claim it appears in says something about all members of the class in question. "All dogs are mammals" distributes the term "dog" because it speaks of all dogs. This A-claim states the same thing about all dogs, that all dogs are mammals. The same claim does not distribute "mammal," because it does not tell you the same thing about all mammals. It does not tell you that all mammals are dogs or that all mammals are not dogs. Hence, the subject term of an A-claim is distributed but not the predicate term of an A-claim. For E-claims, both the subject and the predicate terms are distributed. For example, the sentence "No dogs are cats" says something about all dogs (that they are not cats) and all cats (that they are not dogs). For an I-claim, neither of the terms is distributed. With an O-claim, only the predicate term is distributed. The sentence "Some dogs are not collies" says something about all collies, specifically that all collies are not a particular dog. The distributed terms for each categorical claim are in **boldface and are underlined** below.

A: All **<u>S</u>** are P.

E: No **<u>S</u>** are **<u>P</u>**.

I: Some S are P.

O: Some S are not **<u>P</u>**.

With this terminology in place, we can state the four rules. A categorical syllogism is valid if it obeys **The Four Rules:**

1. The middle term is distributed in at least one of the premises.
2. All terms distributed in the conclusion are distributed in the premises.
3. The number of negative premises is the same as the number of negative conclusions.
4. There are not two universal premises and a particular conclusion.

A syllogism is invalid if it breaks Rules 1, 2, or 3. If a syllogism does not break any of the four rules, then it is a valid argument.

Example One
No **women are fathers.**
All **mothers** are women.
No **mothers are fathers.**

Example Two
Some women are mothers.
Some mothers are cooks.
No **cooks** are **women**.

In the above examples, the terms that are distributed are in boldface. **Example One** is valid because it does not **break** any of the rules. Rule 1: The middle term "women" is distributed at least once. Rule 2: The terms that are distributed in the conclusion (e.g., both "mothers" and "fathers") are also distributed in the premises. Rule 3: There is one negative premise, and there is one negative conclusion. Rule 4: You don't have two universal premises followed by a particular conclusion (the conclusion is universal).

Example Two breaks Rules 1–3 and is an invalid argument; breaking any of the first three rules would have been sufficient to invalidate the argument. Rule 1: The middle term "mother" is not distributed at least once. Rule 2: The terms "cooks" and "women" are both distributed in the conclusion, but they are not distributed in the premises. Rule 3: There are zero negative premises and one negative conclusion. Rule 4 is not broken because we have two particular premises followed by a negative conclusion.

If a syllogism violates only Rule 4, the syllogism is conditionally valid, which means that it may still be valid from the Aristotelian standpoint if a particular term denotes actually existing things. One way to identify this particular term is to look it up on the chart (the required condition) or to identify the Venn circle that is almost completely shaded. Another way to identify this term is to find which term is "**superfluously distributed**": the superfluously distributed term (SDT) is the term in one of the premises that is distributed in more occurrences than is necessary for the syllogism to obey all the rules (namely, Rules 1 and 2). Here are some examples where the terms are M, S, and P. The distributed terms are in boldface:

Example Three
All **M** are P.
All **S** are M.
Some S are P.

SDT is S.

Example Four
No **M** are **P**.
All **M** are S.
Some S are not **P**.

SDT is M.

Example Five
All **P** are M.
All **M** are S.
Some S are P.

SDT is P.

For these three arguments, the superfluously distributed terms (SDT) are S, M, and P, respectively. In Example Three, the two terms distributed in the premises are M and S. By Rule 1, the term M had to be distributed since the middle term must be distributed at least once in a premise; however, term S did not have to be distributed by either Rules 1 or 2. In Example Four, we have three distributed terms in the premises, both occurrences of M and the term P. By Rule 2, the term P had to be distributed in the premise because it is distributed in the conclusion. Rule 1 only requires the middle term to be distributed at least once, but the middle term is distributed twice. Thus, M is superfluously distributed. Finally, in Example Five, the term P did not have to be distributed by Rules 1 or 2. After identifying the superfluously distributed term, we then ask whether it actually exists. If the superfluously distributed term exists, then the syllogism is valid. If it does not exist, then the syllogism commits the existential fallacy and is invalid from the Aristotelian as well as the Boolean standpoint.

Let's apply the four rules to these two examples where the terms denote specific things. The distributed terms are in boldface.

Example Six
All **gems** are diamonds.
All **diamonds** are stones.
Some stones are gems.

Example Seven
No **fairies** are **mermaids**.
All **mermaids** are rational creatures.
Some rational creatures are not **fairies**.

For Example Six, only Rule 4 is broken. The superfluously distributed term is gems because the middle term, diamonds, had to be distributed at least once according to Rule 1.

For Example Seven, only Rule 4 is broken. The superfluously distributed term is mermaid because it only had to be distributed once to follow Rule #1, but the middle term is distributed twice in the premises. The term "fairies" is not superfluously distributed because Rule 2 states that a term distributed in the conclusion has to be distributed in the premise.

Exercise 6-B Four Rules Method

Apply the rules method to the following categorical syllogisms to determine validity. Your final answers should match the answers from the previous exercise.

1. All marsupials are animals.
   All koalas are marsupials.
   All koalas are animals.

2. Some cities are state capitals.
   All state capitals are familiar places.
   Some familiar places are cities.

3. All dictionaries are books.
   No dictionaries are comics.
   All comics are books.

4. Some dictionaries are books.
   Some paper goods are not books.
   Some paper goods are dictionaries.

5. All stallions are horses.
   <u>Some pets are not horses.</u>
   Some pets are not stallions.

6. Some lawyers are not politicians.
   <u>All senators are politicians.</u>
   Some senators are not lawyers.

7. Some warriors are not men.
   <u>All actors are men.</u>
   All actors are warriors.

8. Some gems are diamonds.
   <u>All diamonds are stones.</u>
   Some stones are gems.

9. No werewolves are athletes.
   <u>All werewolves are professionals.</u>
   Some professionals are not athletes.

10. No cherries are apples.
    <u>Some strawberries are not apples.</u>
    No strawberries are cherries.

11. Some furniture are not tables.
    <u>Some tables are not desks.</u>
    All desks are furniture.

12. No humans are genies.
    <u>All genies are rational creatures.</u>
    Some rational creatures are not humans.

13. All leprechauns are millionaires.
    <u>No paupers are millionaires.</u>
    Some paupers are not leprechauns.

14. 14. All pixies are sprites.
    <u>No bees are sprites.</u>
    Some bees are not pixies.

15. Some ballerinas are not wrestlers.
    <u>All ballerinas are dancers.</u>
    Some dancers are not wrestlers.

16. No free acts are caused actions.
    <u>All human acts are caused actions.</u>
    So, no human acts are free acts.

17. All gymnasts are athletes.
    <u>Some dancers are gymnasts.</u>
    Some dancers are athletes.

18. All geniuses are smart persons.
    <u>All wizards are geniuses.</u>
    Some wizards are smart persons.

19. Some shoes are boots.
    <u>Some gloves are not shoes.</u>
    No gloves are boots.

20. All bats are winged creatures.
    <u>All winged creatures are fairies.</u>
    Some fairies are bats.

21. All vampires are carnivores.
    All vampires are garlic haters.
    Some garlic haters are carnivores.

22. All dogs are canines.
    No canines are felines.
    No felines are dogs.

23. All pixies are sprites.
    No sprites are hummingbirds.
    Some hummingbirds are not pixies.

24. No optimists are skeptics.
    All leprechauns are optimists.
    Some leprechauns are not skeptics.

CHAPTER 7
Propositional Logic

> In Chapter 7, we will learn a symbolic language called propositional or sentential logic to evaluate deductive reasoning.
> - Identify well-formed formulas of propositional logic
> - Translate English sentences into propositional logic
> - Translate well-formed formulas of propositional logic into English sentences

Propositional logic is a precise and useful method for testing the validity of arguments. Also called sentential logic, propositional logic is the logic of sentences. It has applications as wide-ranging as set theory and the fundamental principles of computer science, as well as being useful for the examination of ordinary arguments. Finally, the precision of truth-functional logic makes it a good introduction to nonmathematical symbolic systems.

This chapter explains how to symbolize the complex arrangements of individual sentences expressed in ordinary language. We will use letters to represent atomic statements, the simplest kind of sentence in propositional logic. Also, a few special symbols called **logical connectives** or **operators** will represent the standard relations among sentences, relations that correspond to English words such as "not," "and," "or," and "if-then." Truth tables show how the truth-values of the individual claims determine the truth-values of their compounds.

Propositional logic is a **truth-functional** logic because the truth-value of a more complex sentence depends on the truth-values of its component parts or atomic statements. An atomic statement expresses one complete thought and is symbolized by a capital letter in propositional logic. This differs from categorical logic where we use capital letters to represent terms (plural nouns or noun phrases) rather than to represent atomic statements. Every atomic statement has a truth-value, true or false. We use T and F to represent the two possible truth-values.

When the truth-value of an atomic statement is unknown, we may use a truth table to indicate all possibilities. Thus, for a single letter P, we write:

P
T
F

Any atomic statement may be true or false; its **negation** (contradictory claim) will have the opposite truth-value. Using ~P to mean the negation of P, we produce the following truth table:

P	~P
T	F
F	T

This truth table is a definition of negation. ~P is read "not-P." This is our first truth-functional connective or **logical operator**. The negation logical operator is called the tilde. The tilde is the only one of our five logical operators that is **unary**; it precedes one sentence which it negates. The remaining truth-functional symbols cover relations between two sentences and are known as **binary** operators. Each symbol corresponds, more or less, to an ordinary English word, but you will find the symbols clearer and more rigid than their ordinary-language counterparts. Accordingly, each logical operator receives a precise definition within a truth table and never deviates from that definition.

A **conjunction** "P and Q" is translated by using the logical symbol, the dot •. Like the tilde ~, the dot is used to form compound sentences; however, it is a binary operator because it connects two simper statements or conjuncts. A conjunction asserts that both of the simpler claims contained in it are true. That is, a conjunction is true if and only if both of the simpler claims or conjuncts are true. We write:

P	Q	P•Q
T	T	T
T	F	F
F	T	F
F	F	F

Notice that this truth table needs four lines, not two, to capture all the possible truth-values of P and Q. There is only one way for a conjunction to come out true but many ways for it to come out false. Although the standard way to express a conjunction in English is by the word "and," other words can communicate conjunctions: "but," "although," "while," "even though," "yet," "however," "nevertheless," "despite," etc. "And" sometimes has connotations that • lacks. "I had dinner and went to bed" suggests that one thing happened before the other; the logical conjunction carries no such suggestion. Likewise, the words "but" or "however" often implies that the second conjunct is surprisingly true even though the first conjunct is true.

Sometimes, punctuation such as a comma or a semicolon can express conjunction. The following examples leave out the conjunctive word such as "and," "but," or "yet." We may translate them nevertheless as a conjunction using the "•" logical connective.

The following are quotes that contain negations and conjunctions. The translation in propositional logic precedes the quote, and the capital letters used to represent the atomic statements are underlined and boldface.

~S	You cannot **s**tep into the same river twice. —Heraclitus
~K	Science does not **k**now its debt to imagination. —Ralph Waldo Emerson
(P • C)	I will **p**repare and some day my **c**hance will come. —Abraham Lincoln
(H • A)	We **h**ang the petty thieves and **a**ppoint the great ones to public office. —Aesop
(F • T)	I'm **f**at, but I'm **t**hin inside. —George Orwell
(V • M)	Virtue has a **v**eil, vice a **m**ask. —Victor Hugo
(D • H)	Man needs **d**ifficulties; they are necessary for **h**ealth. —Carl Jung
(S • O)	Although the world is full of **s**uffering, it is also full of **o**vercoming of it. —Helen Keller
(~L • R)	It is not **l**iving that matters, but living **r**ightly. —Socrates
(S • C)	Being deeply loved by someone give you **s**trength, while loving someone deeply gives you **c**ourage. —Lao Tzu
(B • ~M)	Friends are **b**orn, not **m**ade. —Henry Adams
(~C • A)	Kind words do not **c**ost much, yet they **a**ccomplish much. —Blaise Pascal

A third type of sentence is a **disjunction**, such as the phrase "Either P or Q," which may be symbolized using the wedge ∨. "Either P or Q" is translated as (P ∨ Q) in propositional logic. (P ∨ Q) is a compound sentence asserting either or both of the simpler statements contained in it. More precisely, we say that a disjunction is false if and only if both of the simpler claims are. The truth table is similar to the one for conjunction.

P	Q	P ∨ Q
T	T	T
T	F	T
F	T	T
F	F	F

Aside from the different arrangement of truth-values in the final column, this table is set up like the last one. It's as hard to make a disjunction false as it is to make a conjunction true. "Or" as symbolized by the wedge represents the **inclusive sense** of "or" where both disjuncts may be true at the same time. As in the example, "You are qualified for the job if you either have a master's degree or five years' work experience." If you happen to have both the degree and experience, you would still be qualified. The wedge does not express the **exclusive sense** of "or" as in the sentence, "You may take the lottery prize in a lump sum or receive payments over the next 20 years." Here the choice is an either/or proposition that excludes the possibility of having both options. The logical disjunction, expressed by the wedge Ú, is inclusive and never forces us to choose between the two disjuncts. Other English words, like "unless," may also be translated into disjunctions.

(P ∨ R)   Art is either **p**lagiarism or **r**evolution. —Paul Gauguin
(G ∨ L)   Mankind is made **g**reat or **l**ittle by its own will. —Friedrich Schiller
(~K ∨ M) You never **k**now what is enough unless you know what is **m**ore than enough. —William Blake

A **conditional statement** (if-then) is translated using the symbol ⊃ called the horseshoe or hook. A conditional is a compound sentence that connects two statements. Recall that the parts of a conditional statement include the antecedent, which usually follows the word "if" and the consequent that follows "then." In the conditional statement (P ⊃ Q), P is the **antecedent**, and Q is the **consequent**. A conditional asserts the consequent is true on the condition that the antecedent is true. A conditional claim is false if and only if its antecedent is true and its consequent is false, as we see in the second row of this truth table.

P	Q	P ⊃ Q
T	T	T
T	F	F
F	T	T
F	F	T

We read "(P ⊃ Q)" as "If P, then Q." In many cases, the logical conditional will strike you as different from the ordinary English "if-then" construction. The essence of our definition is that the conditional only must be false under one set of circumstances: when the antecedent sets up a promised condition and the consequent does not deliver on it. There are many ways to translate the horseshoe in English sentences, and we will introduce several guidelines for translating conditionals in the next section.

A **biconditional** or **equivalence sentences**, translated by the triple bar ≡, is a compound claim asserting that the sentences on either side of the triple bar are logically equivalent; that is, both sides have the same truth-value. The truth table for a biconditional statement reflects that the statement is true when both sides are true and when both sides are false:

P	Q	P ≡ Q
T	T	T
T	F	F
F	T	F
F	F	T

We read "(P ≡ Q)" as "P if and only if Q," "P is equivalent to Q," "P is a necessary and sufficient condition for Q," and "P just in case Q."

These truth tables indicate all the truth-value possibilities for a given compound formula, even if the truth-values of the atomic components or capital letters are unknown. Thus, all the logical operators may be defined truth-functionally since that the truth-value of the compound statement is a function of its atomic parts.

Formulas may contain any number of logical operators. All well-formed formulas (except trivial formulas that contain no operators) contain exactly one **main operator**. The main operator is the operator that is used to obtain the truth-value of the compound proposition represented by the formula. When a formula contains only one operator, that operator is the main operator. It is more difficult to identify the main operator when a formula contains multiple operators; the general procedure for identifying the main operator will be discussed in the next section.

The first significant step in analyzing and operating on claims with truth-functional logic is the work of **translating** them into symbolic form. Ultimately there is no substitute for a careful examination of what the sentences are saying. Translating a compound claim into symbolic form means making its internal logical relations clear and precise. Because ordinary language often gives us compounds with implied or submerged logical relations, we have to begin by making sure we know what they mean.

Conditional statements are perhaps the most challenging to translate because of the variety of ways the same proposition can be expressed in English. The following five rules can guide this translation.

Rule 1: When "**if**" appears by itself, what immediately follows is the **antecedent of the conditional**. In other words, the formula that immediately follows the "if" should go before the horseshoe. Thus, the statements "If **B**ill goes to work, **S**am plays golf" and "**S**am plays golf if **B**ill goes to work" are both translated (B ⊃ S).

Rule 2: When "**only if**" appears, what immediately follows is the **consequent of the conditional**. Therefore, when you see the phrase "only if" and this phrase is not contained in the longer phrase "if and only if," you should put the formula that follows "only if" after the horseshoe. The phrase "if and only if" is translated with a triple bar ≡ to create a biconditional statement.

Some examples can help illustrate Rules 1 and 2.

(K ⊃ J)	**J**ohn goes to the dance if **K**ate accompanies him.
(K ⊃ P)	**K**ate accompanies John only if her **p**arents let her.
(∼T ⊃ M)	If **T**ed does not have to work, then **M**eg will go to the movies with him.

Rule 3: "**Provided**," "**provided that**," "**given that**," "**on condition that**," "**assuming that**" are sometimes used in place of "if." The same rule that governs the word "if" (Rule 1) applies to these phrases. That is, these phrases are followed by the antecedent of a conditional.

(T ⊃ W)   The Dodgers win the **W**orld Series provided they win **t**oday's game.

(P ⊃ N)   Given that the **p**lane arrives on time, we can be home by **n**oon.

Rule 4: The phrases "**entails that**" and "**implies that**" also express conditional statements. These phrases are followed by the consequent and hence are treated in the same way that the phrase "only if" is treated by applying Rule 2.

(R ⊃ M)   **R**ob's being happy entails that (or implies that) **M**egan is happy.

(W ⊃ Q)   Being a **w**riter usually entails a fairly **q**uiet life. —Jill Paton Walsh

Implied in the quote are two simple statements. We will use W to stand for "I am a writer," and Q to mean "I live a fairly quiet life." Walsh's quote may be reexpressed as standard conditional statement, "If I am a writer, then I live a fairly quiet life." In the next example, we will need to convert the words into simple statements in order to translate them into a well-formed formula of propositional logic. Capital letters stand for simple statements, but the words "equality" and "individuality" are not statements that have truth-values. However, we can understand "equality" to mean "there is equality" and "individuality" to mean "there is individuality." Hence, the sentence "Equality implies individuality" is equivalent to saying, "That there is equality implies that there is individuality" or as a conditional, "If there is equality, then there is individuality."

(E ⊃ I)   **E**quality implies **i**ndividuality. —Trey Anastasio

Rule 5: S ⊃ N Sufficient Condition ⊃ Necessary Condition

Another way to express a conditional statement is by the phrase "**is a sufficient condition for**" and "**is a necessary condition for**." Let us consider an example of a true conditional statement:

(E ⊃ S)   If today is **E**aster, then today is **S**unday."

The antecedent of this conditional, "today is Easter," is a sufficient condition for the consequent "today is Sunday." That is, it is enough to know that it is Easter to infer that it is Sunday. Furthermore, the consequent is said to be a necessary condition for the antecedent. In this case, it is necessary that it be Sunday for today to be Easter. The next section will explain more about necessary and sufficient conditions.

"Literacy is a necessary condition for college graduation" means that you must be literate to have graduated from college, though plenty of other things must be true as well. We express this relationship by saying: If you have graduated from college, you are literate (G ⊃ L). Necessary conditions become the consequents of conditionals.

"Being a square is a sufficient condition for being a rectangle" means that if a figure is a square, then it is a rectangle (S ⊃ R). Thus, the sentence "A is a sufficient condition for B" is translated as (A ⊃ B). Whereas, the translation for the sentence "C is a necessary condition for D" is (D ⊃ C).

The expression **"if and only if"** is translated by a triple bar ≡. The shorter way to translate the sentence, "My car will run if and only if you put gas in it," is simply (R ≡ G). This formula is equivalent to a longer translation since the English sentence can be lengthened out to "My car will run if you put gas in it, and my car will run only if you put gas in it." We symbolize the two parts of this longer compound sentence: (G ⊃ C) and (C ⊃ G), respectively. These two sub-formulas may be connected by a dot, resulting in the more complex sentence [(G ⊃ C) • (C ⊃ G)], which is logically equivalent to (G ≡ C). Thus, biconditional statements derive their name because they are equivalent to formulas with two conditionals.

In more complex sentences, the placement of parentheses is important to the overall meaning of the sentence. Henceforth, we will adopt the convention of omitting the outermost parentheses, but inner parentheses must remain to give clarity to some sentences.

Example 1: "Either I will dance and sing, or I will juggle."

Example 2: "I will dance, and I will either sing or juggle."

For these two examples, let us choose D to represent "I will dance," S to represent "I will sing," and J to represent "I will juggle."

Examples 1 and 2 contain the same atomic propositions ("I will dance," "I will sing," "I will juggle") and also the same logical operators (and, or). Yet, it is clear that the two sentences have different meanings. This reflects the fact that the main operators of the two sentences are different. The placement of the word "Either" at the beginning of Example 1 indicates that it is a disjunction. It is translated as

(D • S) ∨ J.

On the other hand, "either" and "or" occur in the middle of Example 2, not the beginning. This is a clue that Example 2 is not a disjunction. Instead, the "and" is the main operator, so Example 2 is a conjunction. It is translated as

D • (S ∨ J).

A similar line of thinking can be used to translate Examples 3 and 4.

Example 3: "If I sing or yodel, then I'll get booed."

Example 4: "I'll sing, or else, if I yodel, I'll get booed."

Again, both the atomic propositions and logical operators are the same. The difference has to do with the main operators. Example 3 begins with the word "if," suggesting that it is a conditional statement. Using a similar naming convention as the prior examples, it is translated as

(S ∨ Y) ⊃ B.

In Example 4, "if" and "then" are embedded within the sentence, suggesting that it is not a conditional statement. This means that the "or" must be the main operator, so Example 4 is a disjunction. It is translated as

S ∨ (Y ⊃ B).

Summary of Main Points

1. Atomic statements are expressed by capital letters.
2. Compound statements are formed by combining capital letters with logical operators.
3. The five logical operators are ∼tilde, • dot, ∨ wedge, ⊃ horseshoe, ≡ triple bar.
4. The tilde is the only unary operator; the other four are binary operators.
5. Translations for

    | Negation | ∼X | "not," "it is false that" |
    | Conjunction | (X • Y) | "and," "but," "however," "yet,"… |
    | Disjunction | (X ∨ Y) | "or," "unless" |

6. Translations for conditional statements "If X, then Y"
   (X ⊃ Y) Antecedent ⊃ Consequent

   "If" is followed by antecedent
   same as "given that," "assuming that," "provided that," "on condition that," …

   "Only if" followed by consequent
   same as "implies that" and "entails that"

   SUN: **S**ufficient Condition ⊃ **N**ecessary condition

7. Translations for biconditional statements
   (X ≡ Y) "X if and only if Y,"
   "X is equivalent to Y,"
   "X is a necessary and sufficient condition for."

8. Outermost parentheses may be omitted.
9. Additional parentheses?
    a. Two binary operators in the same formula must be separated by parentheses.
    b. A well-formed formula must have a main operator.
10. Special translations:
    a. A does not go and B does not go.   ∼A • ∼B
    b. It is not the case that both A and B.   ∼(A • B)

c.	It is not the case that either A or B.	∼(A ∨ B)		
d.	Both A and B do not.	∼A • ∼B		
e.	Neither A nor B.	∼A • ∼B	or	∼(A ∨ B)
f.	Either both A and B go, or C does not go.	(A • B) ∨ ∼C		
g.	Either A or B goes, and C does not go.	(A ∨ B) • ∼C		

Well-Formed Formula (Inductive Definition)

1. Capital letters are well-formed formulas.
2. If X and Y are well-formed formulas, then so are ∼X, (X • Y), (X ∨ Y), (X ⊃ Y), and (X ≡ Y).
3. Nothing else is a WFF.

Exercise 7-A Well-Formed Formulas

Which are WFF's (syntactically correct arrangement of symbols)? If not well-formed, explain why.

1. ∼A • K ∨ (S ⊃ O)
2. D ⊃ (∼Q ≡ pH) • S)
3. (∼B • B) ≡ ∼B
4. ∼(∼∼R ⊃ Y) • (∼J • ∼N)
5. ⊃ C • [(L ⊃ K) ⊃ (I ∼K)]
6. ∼∼[∼G ⊃ P ∨ (∼D • Z)]
7. ∼K ⊃ [∼E ∨ ∼J • S]
8. ∼C • [∼(L ∨ C) ⊃ ∼(∼M ⊃ N)]

Exercise 7-B Propositional Logic Translations

Translate these sentences into well-formed formulas of propositional logic.

1. The quick brown fox jumped over the lazy dog.
2. He loves me.
3. He loves me not. He does not love me. It's not the case that he loves me.
4. It's not the case that he does not love me.
5. Amy and Bob went.
6. Four is even, but 9 is odd.
7. Four is even, but 9 is odd and 6 is even.
8. Both 4 and 6 are even, and 9 is odd.
9. New York and California are miles apart.

10. Spot is a good dog, yet he just mauled your cat.
    Spot is a good dog, although he just mauled your cat.
    Spot is a good dog, despite that he just mauled your cat.
11. Amy did not go, and Bob did not go.
12. It's false that both Amy and Bob went.
13. Amy went; however, Bob did not.
14. Amy did not go, or Bob did not go.
15. It's not the case that either Amy or Bob went.
16. Amy went, or Bob did not go.
17. Amy went or Bob went, but not both.
18. Neither Amy nor Bob went.
19. If you are a mother, then you are female.
20. You are female if you are a mother.
21. You are a mother only if you are female.
22. Amy's going is a sufficient condition for Bob's going.
23. Amy's going is a necessary condition for Bob to go.
24. If today is not Monday, tomorrow is not Tuesday.
25. Tomorrow is not Sunday if today is Monday.
26. Today's being Monday implies that tomorrow is Tuesday.
27. Provided that tomorrow is Tuesday, I will wash and wax the car.
28. Today is Halloween if it's October 31, and today is Halloween only if it's October 31.
29. Today is Halloween if and only if it is October 31.
30. Today being Halloween is a necessary and sufficient condition for today being October 31.
31. You can use the car tonight only if you wash and wax it this afternoon.
32. You can use the car tonight if and only if you wash and wax it this afternoon.
33. You're damned if you do, and damned if you don't. So, you're damned. (*Translate into two formulas: one premise and one conclusion.*)
34. Sally can't both have the report ready first thing tomorrow and be home by 8:00 tonight. If the report isn't ready, her boss will be disappointed. If she isn't home by 8:00, her husband will be disappointed. So at least one of them will be disappointed. (*Translate into four formulas: three premises, one conclusion.*)
35. Some states (California) administer lethal **i**njection unless the inmate requests lethal **g**as.
36. Some states (Idaho) authorize a **f**iring squad only if lethal **i**njection cannot be given, and some states (New Hampshire) authorize **h**anging only if lethal **i**njection cannot be given.
37. Some states (Washington) provide that lethal **i**njection be administered unless the inmate requests **h**anging; however, some states (South Carolina) allow the prisoners to choose between lethal **i**njection or **e**lectrocution.
38. Some states (Oklahoma) authorize electrocution if lethal **i**njection is not constitutional; however, some states authorize **f**iring squad if both lethal **i**njection and **e**lectrocution are not constitutional.
39. A person is executed by **e**lectrocution in Kentucky, provided that both the capital offense occurred before **M**arch 31, 1998, and the person does not opt for lethal **i**njection.

40. Tanya Faye Tucker's committing a capital offense in **T**exas entails her being lethally **i**njected unless the governor grants her a **p**ardon.
41. Being executed by **h**anging is a sufficient condition for having committed a capital offense in **N**ew Hampshire or **W**ashington.
42. Being **e**lectrocuted is a necessary condition for being executed in **N**ebraska, but being executed by **f**iring squad is a sufficient condition for being executed in **I**daho or in **U**tah.
43. It is not the case that California allows execution by either **f**iring squad or **e**lectrocution.
44. It is not the case that both **H**awaii and **M**issouri permit capital punishment; however, both **H**awaii and **A**laska do not permit capital punishment.
45. Both **T**ennessee and **K**entucky give their inmates a choice of execution methods, but neither **N**ebraska nor **M**ississippi gives their inmates a choice of execution methods.
46. Utah does not execute on either **S**undays or **M**ondays, and **h**olidays are also excluded.

Exercise 7-C Propositional Logic Translations

Use the following scheme of abbreviation to translate sentences into symbols of well-formed formulas of propositional logic.

A: The commander is **a**ble.
B: The army wins the **b**attle.
C: The soldiers **c**onceal their position.
F: The ruler shows **f**oresight.
N: The enemy is **n**ear.
O: The soldiers **o**bey orders explicitly.

1. Either the soldiers obey orders explicitly and conceal their position or the army does not win the battle.
2. The soldiers neither obey orders explicitly nor conceal their positions, although the ruler shows foresight.
3. The army wins the battle or the soldiers obey orders explicitly, but the commander is not able if and only if the enemy is near.
4. It is not the case that both the ruler shows foresight and the commander is able; however, given that the soldiers conceal their position, the army wins the battle.
5. The ruler does not show foresight unless both the commander is able and the army wins the battle.
6. Either the soldiers do not conceal their position or do not obey orders explicitly, provided that the commander is not able.
7. The soldiers obey orders explicitly only if the enemy is near, on the assumption that the ruler does not show foresight.
8. The army's winning the battle implies that the commander is able, and the ruler's showing foresight is a necessary condition for the commander to be able.

76 | Basics of Logic

9. The commander's being able is a sufficient and necessary condition for the army to win the battle; yet, the soldiers' obeying orders explicitly is a sufficient condition for the soldiers' concealing their position.
10. It is not the case that either the army wins the battle or the soldiers both conceal their positions and obey orders explicitly.

Exercise 7-D Translating Famous Quotes

Translate these famous quotes into well-formed formulas of propositional logic.

1. If you tell the **t**ruth, you don't have to **r**emember anything. —Mark Twain
2. You may **d**elay, but **t**ime will not. —Benjamin Franklin
3. Anger cannot be dis**h**onest. —Marcus Aurelius
4. **A**bsence sharpens love, **p**resence strengthens it. —Thomas Fuller
5. A woman must have **m**oney and a **r**oom of her own if she is to **w**rite fiction. —Virginia Woolf
6. On the whole, human beings want to be **g**ood, but not **t**oo good, and not quite **a**ll the time. —George Orwell
7. Knowledge rests not upon **t**ruth alone, but upon **e**rror also. —Carl Jung
8. If there is no **G**od, everything is **p**ermitted. —Fyodor Dostoevsky
9. I am always ready to **l**earn although I do not always like being **t**aught. —Winston Churchill
10. The man of knowledge must be able not only to **l**ove his enemies but also to **h**ate his friends. —Friedrich Nietzsche
11. I am neither a **m**an nor a **w**oman but an **a**uthor. —Charlotte Brontë
12. Things **e**xist only if they can be **m**easured. —Max Planck
13. Only if you have been in the deepest **v**alley, can you ever know how magnificent it is to be on the highest **m**ountain. —Richard M. Nixon
14. A very small degree of **h**ope is sufficient to cause the birth of **l**ove. —Stendhal
15. It is necessary to have **w**ished for death in order to **k**now how good it is to live. —Alexandre Dumas
16. Three can keep a **s**ecret, if two of them are **d**ead. —Benjamin Franklin
17. This is im**p**ossible only if you **b**elieve it is. —Lewis Carroll
18. All is **w**ell, provided the **l**ight returns and the eclipse does not become endless **n**ight. —Victor Hugo
19. Assuming either the **L**eft Wing or the **R**ight Wing gained control of the country, it would probably fly around in **c**ircles. —Pat Paulsen
20. Increasing **j**obs more than output implies a fall in **p**roductivity and **s**tandards of living. —Alan Greenspan

21. True **f**aith is faith only if the actions of your life are in **h**armony with it and never **c**ontradict it. —Leo Tolstoy
22. **D**emocracy is necessary to **p**eace and to **u**ndermining the forces of terrorism. —Benazir Bhutto
23. Life would be **t**ragic if it weren't **f**unny. —Stephen Hawking
24. A **f**arewell is necessary before you can **m**eet again. —Richard Bach
25. It is not necessary for **e**agles to be **c**rows. —Sitting Bull
26. I am extraordinarily **p**atient, provided I get my own **w**ay in the end. —Margaret Thatcher
27. You can act like a **p**oliceman or a **s**oldier, but not both. —Tom Clancy
28. Success isn't **p**ermanent and **f**ailure isn't fatal. —Mike Ditka
29. I **s**wear like a sailor, assuming the sailor in question **d**ied in 1800 and was **r**eally square. —Alexandra Petri
30. Either **l**ife entails **c**ourage, or it ceases to **b**e life. —E. M. Forster
31. The lonely become either **t**houghtful or **e**mpty. —Mason Cooley
32. The turtle makes **p**rogress only if he sticks his **n**eck out. —James Bryant Conant
33. It isn't necessary to be **r**ich and **f**amous to be **h**appy; it's only necessary to be **r**ich. —Alan Alda
34. If he doesn't **f**ollow through with actions, he's either **s**elfish or a **l**iar. —Matthew Hussey
35. You can **o**vercome anything, if and only if you **l**ove something enough. —Lionel Messi
36. It is amazing what you can **a**ccomplish if you do not **c**are who gets the credit. —Harry S. Truman
37. Marriage is neither **h**eaven nor hel**l**, it is simply **p**urgatory. —Abraham Lincoln
38. There are no **s**trangers here; only **f**riends you haven't yet met. —William Butler Yeats
39. If you're **t**eaching today what you were teaching five years ago, either the **f**ield is dead or **y**ou are. —Noam Chomsky
40. I was taught that the way of progress was neither **s**wift nor **e**asy. —Marie Curie

CHAPTER 8
Truth Tables (Regular or Long Method)

> In Chapter 8, we will apply the truth table method to determine the truth-value of a compound statement. Building on this, we will use the truth table method to classify statements as tautologous, self-contradictory, and contingent statements. This method will also be useful in determining the equivalence and consistency of statements, as well as the validity of arguments.
>
> - Identify the main operator of a compound statement
> - Determine the truth-value of a statement given the truth values of its simple components
> - Classify a statement as being tautologous, self-contradictory, or contingent
> - Compare two statements as being equivalent, contradictory, or neither
> - Determine the consistency of a set of statements
> - Evaluate the validity of arguments

For propositional logic, we can construct a truth table for any well-formed formula. A truth table must capture all possible combinations of truth values for the atomic statements contained in a complex sentence. A truth table is designed to show all the conditions under which a given sentence is true or false.

To construct our truth table, we may begin by creating columns at the left of the table for each of the simple statements represented as capital letters. These are the reference columns. If you have n atomic statements or capital letters in an expression, you will need 2^n rows: one atomic statement or capital letter requires two rows, two capital letters require four rows, three capital letters require 8 rows, four capital letters require 16 rows, and so on. Here are the reference columns for a truth table built to handle three capital letters, P, Q, and R:

P	Q	R
T	T	T
T	T	F
T	F	T
T	F	F
F	T	T
F	T	F
F	F	T
F	F	F

With this truth table containing three atomic sentences, P, Q, and R, the rightmost column alternates T's and F's; the column just to its left goes T-T-F-F; the column to the left of that is T-T-T-T-F-F-F-F, and so on. The leftmost column of a truth table will begin with half the total number of rows being T's and the second half F's. Truth tables may be used to classify a claim as being a tautology (always true), a self-contradiction (always false), or a contingent statement (sometimes true and sometimes false).

When calculating truth values in a truth table, it is important to pay attention to the grouping indicated by the parentheses. Parentheses specify where a truth-functional operation is doing its work. 5 + 3 × 2 makes no sense in arithmetic. It must be written either (5 + 3) × 2, in which case it equals 16, or 5 + (3 × 2), in which case it equals 11. Similarly, the symbols that link the atomic statements make no sense when strung together without separation, as in P • Q ∨ R ⊃ S. Parentheses are needed to show the order of the logical operators. For example, (P • Q) ∨ (R ⊃ S) is a well-formed formula that includes the necessary parentheses for us to understand the sentence.

There are a number of key concepts we need to understand before constructing a truth table. We must know the truth-functional definitions for the five logical operators, the number of rows in a table, the order for plugging in truth values, and the main operator. The key concepts are as follows:

I. Truth-Functional Definitions of Logical Operators
   ∼Opposite truth-value
   • True only when T • T
   ∨ False only when F ∨ F
   ⊃ False only when T ⊃ F
   ≡ True when T ≡ T and F ≡ F

II. The Order for Plugging in Truth Values
   1. Capital letters
   2. Negated letters (∼immediately before letter)
   3. Logical operators inside parentheses
   4. Logical operators outside parentheses
   5. Main operator

III. What Is the Main Operator?
The main operator is the logical operator that lies outside the parentheses, and if there is more than one logical operator outside the parentheses, then the main operator is not the ~tilde.

IV. How many rows are in your truth table? There are 2^n where n is the number of different letters.

V. Which column? = Which one did you enter in last on that side? When deciding which truth values to combine, you should consider which truth values were entered last in particular subformulas.

VI. Classifying Statements
Tautology – all T's under the main column
Self-contradictory – all F's under the main column
Contingent – Some T's and some F's under the main column

Example One		Example Two		Example Three	
A	~A ≡ A	B	B ⊃ ~B	C	~(C • ~C)
T	F T **F** T	T	T **F** F T	T	**T** T F F T
F	T F **F** F	F	F **T** T F	F	**T** F F T F
	⇑ Self-contradiction		⇑ Contingent		⇑ Tautology

Example Four			Example Five		
D	E	~(~D ∨ ~E)	G	H	(~G • H) ⊃ ~G
T	T	**T** F T F F T	T	T	F T F T **T** F T
T	F	**F** F T T T F	T	F	F T F F **T** F T
F	T	**F** T F T F T	F	T	T F T T **T** T F
F	F	**F** T F T T F	F	F	T F F F **T** T F
		⇑ Contingent			⇑ Tautology

Example Six				
M	N	O	~[(M • N) ⊃ (O ∨ N)]	
T	T	T	**F** T T T T T T T	Row 1
T	T	F	**F** T T T T F T T	Row 2
T	F	T	**F** T F F T T T F	Row 3
T	F	F	**F** T F F T F F F	Row 4
F	T	T	**F** F F T T T T T	Row 5
F	T	F	**F** F F T T F T T	Row 6

F	F	T	**F** F F F T T T F	**Row 7**
F	F	F	**F** F F F T F F F	**Row 8**
			⇑ Self-contradiction	

In the previous table, the capital letters have been arranged alphabetically. The question may arise: What if we arrange the letters in a different order? How would that affect our table? Regardless of the order of the statement variables (i.e., the capital letters), the final answer will end up the same; Example Six will still be a self-contradictory sentence. However, if you compare the tables for Examples Six and Seven, you may notice that the rows will be in a slightly different order.

Example Seven				
O	M	N	Same formula as Example Six $\sim[(M \bullet N) \supset (O \vee N)]$	
T	T	T	**F** T T T T T T	Row 1
T	T	F	**F** T F F T T T F	Row 3
T	F	T	**F** F F T T T T T	Row 5
T	F	F	**F** F F F T T T F	Row 7
F	T	T	**F** T T T T F T T	Row 2
F	T	F	**F** T F F T F F F	Row 4
F	F	T	**F** F F T T F T T	Row 6
F	F	F	**F** F F F T F F F	Row 8

Truth tables may also be used to show whether two claims are **logically equivalent**. Let us consider our first claim. Take the sentence "Either Peleg and Queequeg will both go harpooning, or Queequeg won't." We first render it, with obvious symbols, $(P \bullet Q) \vee \sim Q$. The truth table contains two claim variables (two different capital letters "P" and "Q") and thus needs four rows. Note that the complete truth table has not been filled in, just the final main operator column:

P	Q	$(P \bullet Q) \vee \sim Q$
T	T	**T**
T	F	**T**
F	T	**F**
F	F	**T**

Now we can say that the complex expression is false only in Row 3, that is, only when P is false and Q is true. Next, let us consider our second claim "If Queequeg goes harpooning, then Peleg will also," i.e., $Q \supset P$:

P	Q	Q ⊃ P
T	T	**T**
T	F	**T**
F	T	**F**
F	F	**T**

This final column is identical to the final column for "Either Peleg and Queequeg will both go harpooning, or Queequeg won't." The two claims are truth-functionally equivalent. When two expressions containing the same claim variables have identical columns in truth tables, we call them **truth-functionally equivalent**. Two claims are truth-functionally contradictory when the resulting main columns are exactly opposite from one another. For example, Q ⊃ P is logically contradictory to ∼(P ∨ ∼Q).

P	Q	∼(P ∨ ∼Q)
T	T	**F**
T	F	**F**
F	T	**T**
F	F	**F**

Logical consistency is also a property of sets of statements that we can test for by means of the truth table method. A set of statements or beliefs are called consistent if all the statements can possibly be true at the same time. In terms of a truth table, two or more propositions are said to be mutually **consistent** if a truth table containing all the statements has at least one row in which all the propositions have the truth-value T under the main operators. This means that two or more propositions are **inconsistent** if the truth table containing all the statements does not have even one row in which all the statements are true under the main operators.

		I	II	III
P	Q	(P • Q) ∨ ∼Q	Q ⊃ P	∼(P ∨ ∼Q)
T	T	**T**	**T**	**F**
T	F	**T**	**T**	**F**
F	T	**F**	**F**	**T**
F	F	**T**	**T**	**F**

Comparing these same three sentences, we find that Sentences I and II are consistent with Rows 1, 2, and 4. Sentences I and III are inconsistent as well as Sentences II and III. Sentences I, II, and III as a group are also inconsistent. Also, we can claim that Sentences I and III are contradictory to each other. All three sentences separately viewed are contingent statements.

When comparing statements, we should keep in mind these definitions:

Logically Equivalent – main columns of two statements are exactly the same

Logically Contradictory – main columns of two statements are exactly opposite

Logically Consistent – at least one row in which all the statements are true under the main operator

Truth tables offer one method for testing the validity of an argument. This method builds from a single principle, the definition of validity. Recall that for an argument to be valid, it must have a true conclusion whenever all its premises are true. So, we enter all the premises of the argument, and its conclusion, in a truth table, and examine the rows in which all premises are true. If the conclusion is true in all such rows, the argument is valid. If even one row exists in which all premises are true and the conclusion is false, the argument is invalid. A row in a truth table where all the premises are true while the conclusion is false is often called a counterexample. An argument for which a counterexample is possible is an invalid argument. Sometimes all the premises of an argument are never all true in a single row. In that case, the argument is valid, for we have no rows in which all the premises are true and the conclusion false.

Suppose someone offered an argument consisting of the three earlier sentences, with the first two sentences serving as the premises and the last sentence as the conclusion. We would create a long truth table in which the premises are separated by a single slash / and the conclusion by a double slash //.

P	Q	Premise I (P • Q) ∨ ~Q /	Premise II Q ⊃ P //	Conclusion ~(P ∨ ~Q)
T	T	**T**	**T**	**F**
T	F	**T**	**T**	**F**
F	T	**F**	**F**	**T**
F	F	**T**	**T**	**F**

When evaluating the validity of arguments, these definitions are important:

Invalid argument – there is at least one counterexample or "invalidating" row, a row in which all the premises are true, and the conclusion is false under the main operators. ←☹

Valid argument – there is no counterexample or "invalidating" row anywhere on the truth table.

The previous argument contains three invalidating rows (Rows 1, 2, & 4) in which all the premises are true while the conclusion is false under the main operators. Although this argument contains three invalidating rows, just one invalidating row would be enough to make the whole argument invalid. In this next example, there is only one premise, and the second statement is the conclusion. We see that in Row 1, the one premise is true while the conclusion is false. Because of Row 1, this argument is invalid.

		Premise I		Conclusion	
P	Q	(P • Q) ∨ ~Q	//	~Q	
T	T	**T**		**F**	☹
T	F	**T**		**T**	
F	T	**F**		**F**	
F	F	**T**		**T**	

Here's an example of a valid argument. There is not a single row in which all the premises are true while the conclusion is false. In this example, there are two premises and one conclusion.

		Premise I		Premise II		Conclusion
P	Q	Q ∨ ~Q	/	Q ⊃ P	//	~(P ∨ ~Q)
T	T	**F**		**T**		**F**
T	F	**F**		**T**		**F**
F	T	**F**		**F**		**T**
F	F	**F**		**T**		**F**

In this last example, we have three premises followed by a conclusion. We should be able to tell that it is an invalid argument because of Row 2 in which the three premises are true and the conclusion is false.

B	~(B • (B ≡ B))	/	B ≡ B	/	~B ⊃ ~B	//	~~B
T	**F**		**T**		**T**		**T**
F	**T**		**T**		**T**		**F**

Before constructing a truth table, we will begin by calculating the truth tables of compound statements given the truth values of its component simple statements (i.e., given the truth values of the capital letters).

Example One
Suppose A, B, C are true and X, Y, Z are false, what is the truth-value of

~A • Z
T F

1. Enter the truth values, as stipulated by the directions, under the capital letters.

~A • Z
F T F

2. Enter truth values under tildes that immediately precede a capital letter. Since there is a T under A, the negation of A is F. So, we write F under the tilde.

~A • Z
F T **F** F

3. Enter truth values under the main operator (since there are no other symbols or parentheses). We write an F under the dot because there is an F under ~ and an F under the Z. The dot will connect the last truth-value entered on the left side of the dot and the last truth-value entered on the right side of the dot. The answer is that the formula ~A • Z is false. Although we worked this problem out in stages, we normally just write one row of truth values to determine the truth-value of a compound sentence.

Example Two

Suppose A, B, C are true and X, Y, Z are false, what is the truth-value of

~(B ⊃ ~C)
  T   **T**

1. Enter truth values, as stipulated by the directions, under the capital letters.

~(B ⊃ ~C)
  T **F** T

2. Enter truth values under tildes that immediately precede a capital letter. Since there is a T under C, the negation of C is F. So, we write F under the tilde.

~(B ⊃ ~C)

  T **F** F T

3. After entering all the capital letters and negated letters, the next step is to enter values for connectives remaining within the parentheses. We should save the main operator for last, so we should enter F under the horseshoe since B is T and ~C is F.

~(B ⊃ ~C)
T T F F T

Finally, we enter a truth-value under the main operator. Since there are no other logical operators outside of the parentheses, the main operator is the tilde. The main operator tilde takes the opposite of the last truth-value entered within the parentheses. So, it will take the opposite of the F under the horseshoe. Thus, we enter a T under the main operator tilde. The answer is true for this sentence given that B is T and C is T.

Example Three

Suppose A, B, C are true and X, Y, Z are false, what is the truth-value of

~X ≡ (C ∨ Y) F T F	1. Enter truth values, as stipulated by the directions, under the capital letters.
~X ≡ (C ∨ Y) **T** F T F	2. Enter truth values under tildes that immediately precede a capital letter. Since there is an F under X, the negation of X is T. So, we write T under the tilde.
~X ≡ (C ∨ Y) T F T**T**F	3. After entering all the capital letters and negated letters, the next step is to enter values for connectives remaining within the parentheses. Under the wedge, we should enter T since C is T and Y is F.
~X ≡ (C ∨ Y) T F**T** T T F	4. Finally, we enter a truth-value under the main operator. The main operator is the **triple bar**. For the triple bar, we will connect the last truth-value entered on the left of the triple bar and the last truth-value entered on its right side. So, the T under ~X and the T under the wedge will determine the truth-value under the triple bar, making the truth-value for the compound sentence true.

Exercise 8-A Determine Truth Values

Determine the truth values for these well-formed formulas. Let the values for A, B, C be true and the values for X, Y, Z be false.

1. A ∨ ~B
2. ~(A • X)
3. ~(~A ≡ ~C)
4. ~X ⊃ ~B
5. ~(X ⊃ ~Z)
6. ~(~Z ∨ ~C)
7. ~(Y ≡ C)
8. ~X ∨ ~B
9. (~B • ~X) ⊃ Y
10. ~C ≡ ~(X ⊃ ~Z)
11. Y ∨ (~C ≡ X)
12. ~(B • X) ≡ ~C
13. A • (~B • C)
14. C ⊃ (~Z ⊃ Y)
15. ~X ∨ ~(B ≡ C)
16. ~(A ⊃ X) ∨ ~Z
17. (Z ⊃ X) ⊃ (~Y • C)
18. ~[(B • Y) ⊃ ~C]
19. ~C ∨ ~(~B ⊃ Z)
20. ~[~Z ∨ (B • ~C)]
21. ~(~A ≡ B) ∨ ~(X ⊃ ~Y)
22. ~[(~B ⊃ C) ⊃ ~Y] • (Z ≡ ~A)

Exercise 8-B Classify Statements (Two Rows)

Construct a truth table for each well-formed formula. Classify each formula as tautologous, self-contradictory, or contingent. Then compare the two formulas in each row (e.g., 1 and 2, 3 and 4). Are they logically equivalent, contradictory, or neither? Are they consistent or inconsistent?

1. J ∨ ~J

2. ~J ⊃ J

3. ~K ≡ K

4. ~(K ⊃ ~K)

5. ~(L • ~L)

6. ~(~L ≡ ~L)

7. (~M ∨ M) ⊃ ~M

8. ~M • ~(M ≡ ~M)

9. ~[N • (N ⊃ N)]

10. ~(N ∨ ~N) ⊃ N

Exercise 8-C Classify Statements (Four Rows)

Construct a truth table for each well-formed formula. Is each formula tautologous, self-contradictory, or contingent? Is each pair of formulas equivalent, contradictory, consistent, or inconsistent?

11. ~A ∨ ~B

12. ~(A • B)

13. ~C • (~D • C)

14. C ⊃ (~C ⊃ D)

88 | Basics of Logic

15. I ∨ ∼(J ≡ I)

16. ∼(I ⊃ J) • ∼J

17. (K ⊃ L) ∨ (∼K ∨ L)

18. ∼[(K • ∼L) ⊃ L]

Exercise 8-D Classify Statements (Eight Rows)

Construct a truth table for each well-formed formula. Determine whether the formula is tautologous, self-contradictory, or contingent. Then compare each pair of formulas. Determine whether the pair is equivalent, contradictory, consistent, or inconsistent.

19. A ⊃ ∼(∼B • C)

20. ∼[A • ∼(∼B ∨ ∼C)]

21. (∼G ≡ H) • ∼I

22. (G • H) ⊃ (G ∨ I)

23. ∼[D ⊃ (E ⊃ ∼F)]

24. ∼(F ⊃ ∼E) ⊃ ∼D

Exercise 8-E Truth Table for Arguments

Construct a truth table for each argument. Is the argument valid or invalid? Are all the sentences in the argument consistent or inconsistent?

1. ∼A ⊃ ∼B   /   ∼A   //   ∼B

2. ∼A ⊃ ∼B   /   ∼B   //   ∼A

3. C ⊃ C   /   ∼C   //   C ∨ ∼C

4. ∼(J ∨ K)   /   K • ∼J   /   ∼J   //   ∼K ⊃ J

5. E ∨ (F • ∼E)   /   ∼F   //   E ⊃ ∼E

6. G ≡ H   /   ∼H   //   ∼H ≡ I

7. ∼(D ∨ ∼D)   //   D ≡ ∼D

8. ∼N ∨ O   /   ∼(P ≡ N)   //   P • (N ≡ ∼O)

9. (L ∨ M) ⊃ M   //   M ∨ ∼(L ⊃ ∼M)

10. (R • S) ⊃ (R ∨ S)   /   ∼S ≡ R   //   S • ∼(S ⊃ ∼S)

11. ∼(T ∨ ∼T) ≡ T   //   ∼U ⊃ [T • (U ≡ ∼T)]

12. ∼(Q • Q) ∨ (Q ⊃ ∼Q)   /   Q ≡ ∼(Q • ∼Q)   //   ∼Q ⊃ Q

13. ∼(S ⊃ ∼S)   /   ∼S ≡ ∼S   /   S   //   ∼S • (S ∨ ∼S)

14. ∼(K ∨ L) ≡ M   /   ∼(M ∨ ∼L)   //   ∼(K ⊃ ∼L)

CHAPTER 9
Natural Deduction
Four Implication Rules

The method of natural deduction is another way of demonstrating an argument's validity. We begin with the set of premises and apply rules from Group I and Group II (see the following sections) to derive the conclusion. When we generate a new formula in our proof, we write the previous lines used in producing it, along with the abbreviation of the applied rule. This is called the annotation or justification for the deduction.

I. Implication Rules (Group I Rules)

Elementary valid argument patterns constitute the first set of rules for carrying out derivations. We have already been introduced to these patterns, such as modus ponens and modus tollens, in Chapter 2. These valid argument patterns will be the basis for our implication rules or rules of inference. Applying these implication rules will allow us to conclude a new formula from previous ones in our proof. Implication rules are truth-preserving in the sense that if the premises of a proof are true, then any derived lines obtained through the application of the rules will also be true. These apply only to whole lines of a deduction, not to the individual parts of lines. That is, we must deal with the main operators before working on the subformulas (i.e., the formulas within inner parentheses).

Modus ponens (MP; rule 1): Given a conditional in one line of a deduction, and the antecedent to that conditional in another line, we can deduce the consequent. We begin by looking for the antecedent on its own line.

X ⊃ Y	Examples:	(A • B) ⊃ ~C	~D ⊃ (E ∨ ~F)
X		A • B	~D
Y		~C	E ∨ ~F

Note, in the examples, the antecedent or the consequent may be more complex than a single letter. In order to apply MP, the horseshoe ⊃ must be the main operator, and the antecedent of the conditional must appear on its own separate line before the consequent may be derived.

Thus, these would be incorrect applications of MP, and we cannot derive the third formula from the two previous lines.

Incorrect applications of MP:

(A ⊃ B) • (C ⊃ D)   (A • B) ⊃ ∼C
A   ∼C
―――   ―――
B   A • B

Modus tollens (MT; rule 2): Given a conditional claim and the denial of its consequent, we can deduce the denial of the antecedent. We look for the opposite or negation of a consequent on a separate line.

X ⊃ Y   Examples: (A ∨ B) ⊃ D   ∼D ⊃ (E • ∼G)
∼Y   ∼D   ∼(E • ∼G)
―――   ―――――   ――――――
∼X   ∼(A ∨ B)   ∼∼D or D

In these examples, the consequents of the conditional statement are D and (E • ∼G). On a separate line as additional premises, we find the negations of the consequents, respectively: ∼D and ∼(E • ∼G). This allows us to derive the opposite or negation of the antecedents (A ∨ B) and ∼D. For the negation of (A ∨ B), we simply add a ∼ in front of the formula, giving us ∼(A ∨ B). The negation of ∼D may be written as ∼∼D or shortened by double negation to simply D.

Just like MP, the rule MT is a rule of implication applying to the whole formula where the horseshoe ⊃ is the main operator. The following would be incorrect applications of MT:

Incorrect applications of MT:

(A ⊃ B) • (C ⊃ D)   (A • B) ⊃ ∼C
∼B   ∼(A • B)
―――   ―――――
∼A   ∼C

Hypothetical syllogism (HS; rule 3) applies when the consequent of one conditional is the antecedent of another. For HS, we search for a diagonal match.

X ⊃ Y   Examples: A ⊃ ∼B   (D ∨ E) ⊃ ∼F
Y ⊃ Z   ∼B ⊃ C   G ⊃ (D ∨ E)
―――   ―――――   ――――――
X ⊃ Z   A ⊃ C   G ⊃ ∼F

For one example, ∼B is the consequent of one conditional and the antecedent of the other. If we draw a line through the ∼B's, we form a diagonal. The diagonal may also be situated the other way, as in the second example where the two matching formulas are (D ∨ E). We might imagine canceling out the diagonal match between the two conditionals. We then may derive a third conditional, which combines the remaining antecedent and consequent. So, after canceling out ~B, we have left over A and C, which when combined results in the formula A ⊃ C. Note that the position of A and C do not change. A is still the antecedent and C the consequent in the resulting derived formula. Likewise, G and ~F remain the antecedent and consequent, respectively.

These are some incorrect applications of HS. Because this rule is also a rule of implication, the horseshoes of the two previous lines must be the main operators. Also, in the second example, it would be incorrect to switch the places of the subformulas in the antecedent and consequent positions.

Incorrect applications of HS:

(A ⊃ B) • (C ⊃ D)   (A • B) ⊃ ~C   A ⊃ ~B
B ⊃ P   ~C ⊃ D   C ⊃ ~B
A ⊃ P   D ⊃ (A • B)   A ⊃ C

Disjunctive syllogism (DS; rule 4) allows us to infer one of two disjuncts in a disjunction, given the negation of the other disjunct. To apply DS, we must have the denial or opposite of a disjunct in a previous line.

X ∨ Y   or   X ∨ Y   Examples: A ∨ ~B   ~C ∨ (D ⊃ E)
~X   ~Y   ~A   C
Y   X   ~B   D ⊃ E

Thus, given two alternatives, and the denial of one of them, we may derive the other alternative. The alternatives or disjuncts may be atomic letters, negated letters, or longer formulas. We then conclude the other disjunct.

For our examples of incorrect applications of DS, we will again make the illegal move of applying DS when the wedge ∨ is not the main operator. The other incorrect application shown below illegally adds the tilde ~ to the resulting formula.

Incorrect applications of DS:

                                                              A ∨ B
                       (A ∨ B) • (C ⊃ D)   ~A
                       ~A   ~B
                       B

Multistep Proofs Using Rules of Implication

So far, the examples we have seen are applications of a rule to some formulas. We now turn to proofs that involve the application of a number of inference rules toward the goal of proving a conclusion. Before we introduce more implication rules, let us work out a few proofs. Actual proofs will require that we apply a number of rules to derive the desired conclusion. Let's begin with a proof problem that can be solved given the first rule MP. The first three lines represent three premises. A typical proof will begin with one or more premises. The formula after the slash / is the conclusion that we will try to derive. In the following problem, we are asked to derive ∼C from the other formulas.

1. ∼P ⊃ S
2. ∼P
3. S ⊃ ∼C   / ∼C

Begin by scanning the formulas for repeated letters and for main operators. ∼P is shared by both lines 1 and 2, and line 2 has a horseshoe ⊃ as its main operator. Familiarity with MP will prompt you to apply MP to lines 1 and 2, resulting in the formula S. This move is written out as line 4 below. Next to the formula, we provide our justification: the lines used and the abbreviation of the rule.

1. ∼P ⊃ S
2. ∼P
3. S ⊃ ∼C   / ∼C
4. S   1, 2 MP

After that, again scan the lines we have, including the newly added line 4, for repeated letters and main operators. It appears that you can again apply MP, this time to lines 3 and 4.

1. ∼P ⊃ S
2. ∼P
3. S ⊃ ∼C   / ∼C
4. S   1, 2 MP
5. ∼C   3, 4 MP

Each time we add a line to a proof, we number the line, write the resulting derived formula, and justify the step by noting the previous lines and the rule of inference used. We are done with the proof when we have derived the conclusion in our last line. With practice, we will be able to apply any of the 18 rules of inference to solve a proof. The following example illustrates a proof that applies four different rules.

1. (∼J ⊃ O) ⊃ (P ⊃ J)
2. J ∨ (∼J ⊃ O)
3. J ⊃ E
4. ∼E   / P ⊃ E
5. ∼J   3, 4, MT
6. ∼J ⊃ O   2, 5, DS
7. P ⊃ J   1, 6, MP
8. P ⊃ E   3, 7, HS

Line 5

J ⊃ E		X ⊃ Y
~E		~Y
~J	← MT →	~X

Line 6

J ∨ (~J ⊃ O)		X ∨ Y
~J		~X
~J ⊃ O	← DS →	Y

Line 7

(~J ⊃ O) ⊃ (P ⊃ J)		X ⊃ Y
~J ⊃ O		X
P ⊃ J	← MP →	Y

Line 8

P ⊃ J		X ⊃ Y
J ⊃ E		Y ⊃ Z
P ⊃ E	← HS →	X ⊃ Z

Natural Deduction: More Implication Rules

The next four implication rules are also truth-preserving and apply only to the main operators of well-formed formulas.

Constructive dilemma (CD; rule 5) begins with two conditional claims and the disjunction of their antecedents, and moves to the disjunction of their consequents:

(W ⊃ X) • (Y ⊃ Z)
W ∨ Y
X ∨ Z

Example:

(~A ⊃ B) • (C ⊃ ~D)
~A ∨ C
B ∨ ~D

CD looks complicated, but we can think of it as involving two applications of MP. Each set of parentheses contains a conditional statement. The disjunctive statement is the other formula whose disjuncts are the antecedents of the conditionals. MP allows us to derive the consequent of the conditional if we have the antecedent. For CD, we conclude the disjunction of the consequents given the disjunction of the <u>antecedents</u>. In the example, ∼A ∨ C contain the two antecedents. The conclusion results in the formula B ∨ ∼D, which is the disjunction of the consequents.

Incorrect Application of CD:
(∼G ⊃ ∼H) • (∼J ⊃ K)
<u>∼H ∨ K</u>
∼G ∨ ∼J

Incorrect Application of CD:
(∼G ∨ ∼H) • (∼J ∨ K)
<u>∼G ⊃ ∼J</u>
∼H ⊃ K

Simplification (Simp; rule 6) begins with a conjunction. Because a conjunction asserts that both of its conjuncts are true, we can conclude that either of the conjuncts is true. Thus, we begin with just one formula whose main operator is a dot •, and we may derive either conjunct. That is, we may conclude the formula to the left of the main operator dot or to the right of the main operator dot.

<u>X • Y</u>   or   <u>X • Y</u>
X   Y

Examples:

<u>∼A • ∼B</u>   or   <u>∼A • ∼B</u>   <u>(∼C • D) • ∼E</u>   or   <u>(∼C • D) • ∼E</u>
∼A   ∼B   ∼C • D   ∼E

Conjunction (Conj; rule 7), as its name implies, takes any two separate lines of a deduction and joins them together with the dot • as its logical connective. Conj is similar to Simp because the rule involves a main operator dot. Whereas Simp begins with one formula that contains a main operator dot, Conj starts off with two formulas and derives from them a compound formula that contains both previous formulas as its conjunct. This inference is truth-preserving because if two formulas are true, then the conjunction of the two formulas would also be true.

X
<u>Y</u>
X • Y

Examples:

A   C ⊃ D
<u>∼B</u>   <u>E ≡ G</u>
A • ∼B   (E ≡ G) • (C ⊃ D)

Like other implication rules, Simp and Conj begin or end with a dot • as the main operator.

Incorrect Application of Simp:
(A • B) • ~C
A

Incorrect Application of Conj:
~L ∨ N
Q
(~L • Q) ∨ N

Addition (Add; rule 8). Given any line in a deduction, you may create a disjunction that contains that line as one of its disjuncts and anything at all as the other disjunct:

X
X ∨ Y

Examples:

~A
~A ∨ (B • C)

~A ⊃ D
(~A ⊃ D) ∨ ~B

Examples:

A
A ∨ B

~B
~B ∨ ~C

~A
~A ∨ (B • C)

~A ⊃ D
(~A ⊃ D) ∨ ~B

When applying Add, it is important that you end up with a formula whose main operator is a wedge ∨ and not some other logical operator such as a dot •. If we recall that the wedge ∨ represents the inclusive sense of "or," we may understand the legitimacy of this rule of inference. For example, if it is true that we are human, then we could conclude the following statements: we are human or gods; we are human or we are mammals; we are human, or neither cats nor dogs exist. All these statements are true since one of the disjuncts, "we are human," is true. Furthermore, the formula that you join to the previous line in your proof may contain letters that appear in the proof already or letters that do not appear in any previous lines of your proof.

Incorrect Application of Add:
L
L • M

Incorrect Application of Add:
~R • S
(~R ∨ N) • S

In this next example, let us work on a proof that includes CD, Simp, Conj, or Add.

1. (N ⊃ H) • (B ⊃ L)
2. (H ∨ L) ⊃ E
3. (N ∨ B) • ~G   / E ∨ ~K
4. N ∨ B   3, Simp
5. H ∨ L   1, 4, CD

6. E   2, 5, MP
7. E ∨ ~K   6, Add

Line 4

(N ∨ B) • ~G		X • Y
N ∨ B	← Simp →	X

Line 5

(N ⊃ H) • (B ⊃ L)		(W ⊃ X) • (Y ⊃ Z)
N ∨ B		W ∨ Y
H ∨ L	← CD →	X ∨ Z

Line 6

(H ∨ L) ⊃ E		X ⊃ Y
(H ∨ L)		X
E	← MP →	Y

Line 7

E		X
E ∨ ~K	← Add →	X ∨ Y

Let us consider one more short proof:

1. ~R
2. D ⊃ ~(S • ~R)
3. S   / ~D
4. S • ~R   1, 3, Conj
5. ~D   2, 4, MT

Line 4

~R		X
S		Y
S • ~R	← Conj →	X • Y

Line 5

D ⊃ ~(S • ~R)		X ⊃ Y
S • ~R		~Y
~D	← MT →	~X

100 | Basics of Logic

In Exercise 9-A, we will practice simply applying a given rule to some formulas. Then in later exercises, we will work on actual proofs where you must derive the conclusion via multiple steps.

Exercise 9-A Apply Rules of Implication

Apply the rule to the given formulas.

1. **Modus Ponens (MP)**

X ⊃ **Y**	*Conditional (⊃ main operator)*
X	*Antecedent*
Y	*Consequent*

A ⊃ ~B	C ⊃ (C ⊃ D)	~E ⊃ (~F ∨ G)	H • I
A	C	~E	(H • I) ⊃ ~(J ∨ K)

2. **Modus Tollens (MT)**

X ⊃ **Y**	*Conditional (⊃ main operator)*
~**Y**	*Opposite of Consequent*
~**X**	*Opposite of Antecedent*

A ⊃ B	~D ⊃ ~C	(G ≡ ~F) ⊃ E	~(J ∨ K)
~B	C	~E	~H ⊃ (J ∨ K)

3. **Hypothetical Syllogism (HS)**

	X ⊃ **Y**	*Conditional (⊃ main operator)*
Look for a diagonal match	**Y** ⊃ **Z**	*Conditional (⊃ main operator)*
	X ⊃ **Z**	*Conditional (⊃ main operator)*

A ⊃ ~B	D ⊃ E	~(J ∨ K) ⊃ ~L	(O ⊃ ~P) ⊃ ~N
~B ⊃ ~C	(F • G) ⊃ D	~M ⊃ ~(J ∨ K)	~N ⊃ O

4. **Disjunctive Syllogism (DS)**

X ∨ **Y**	**X** ∨ **Y**	*∨ main operator*
~**X**	~**Y**	*Opposite of One Side*
Y	**X**	*Other Side*

| A ∨ B | D ∨ ~C | ~F ∨ E | G ∨ ~H | ~(I ∨ J) |
| ~A | ~D | ~E | H | (I ∨ J) ∨ (L ∨ M) |

5. **Constructive Dilemma (CD)**

	(X ⊃ Y) • (Z ⊃ S)	*Two Conditionals joined by •*
Look for this main structure	**X ∨ Z**	*Two Antecedents joined by ∨*
(⊃) • (⊃)	**Y ∨ S**	*Two Consequents joined by ∨*

| (A ⊃ ~B) • (~C ⊃ D) | (~E ⊃ F) • (~G ⊃ ~H) | ~H ∨ I |
| A ∨ ~C | ~E ∨ ~G | (~H ⊃ ~J) • (I ⊃ ~K) |

6. **Simplification (Simp)**

X • Y   *Take one side of a conjunctive*
X (or Y)   *statement (• main operator)*

Take the first side: *Take the second side:*

| ~A • B | (~D • ~C) • E | (G ∨ ~F) • ~H | L • ~(I • J) |

7. **Conjunction (Conj)**

X   *Connect two previous lines*
Y   *with a dot •*
X • Y

| A | C ⊃ D | ~H | ~X ⊃ ~M |
| ~B | ~E | ~(G ∨ J) | ~N • O |

8. **Addition (Add)**

X   *Attach a wedge ∨ and any formula*
X ∨ Y   *to a previous line*

Add a single letter: *Add a negated letter:*   *Add a compound formula:*

| A | ~B | ~C | D • E | ~G | H ∨ I |

Exercise 9-B Proofs Using Only MP and MT

Apply the Rules of MP and MT to solve the following proofs. Number and justify every line of your proof.

1) 1. J ⊃ K
   2. J   / K

2) 1. B ⊃ C
   2. ~C   / ~B

3) 1. R ⊃ ~S
   2. R   / ~S

4) 1. M ⊃ ~P
   2. ~~P   / ~M

5) 1. ~L ⊃ ~H
   2. ~L   / ~H

6) 1. ~G
   2. ~E ⊃ G   / E

7) 1. ~L ⊃ ~N
   2. E ⊃ N
   3. ~L   / ~E

8) 1. ~S ⊃ C
   2. ~A ⊃ ~S
   3. ~C   / A

9) 1. S
   2. H ⊃ ~S
   3. ~J ⊃ H   / J

10) 1. ~D ⊃ ~N
    2. ~D ⊃ (E ⊃ N)
    3. ~D   / ~E

11) 1. ~P ⊃ (~P ⊃ G)
    2. ~O
    3. ~O ⊃ ~P / G

12) 1. B
    2. B ⊃ (A ⊃ Z)
    3. ~Z   / ~A

13) 1. R ⊃ (R ⊃ ~M)
    2. ~M ⊃ C
    3. R   / C

14) 1. (P ∨ G) ⊃ (~I ⊃ N)
    2. ~N
    3. P ∨ G   / I

15) 1. (Q • E) ⊃ ~R
    2. ~(Q • E) ⊃ J
    3. ~J   / ~R

16) 1. (W • ~L) ⊃ ~N
    2. ~N ⊃ ~J
    3. W • ~L   / ~J

17) 1. ~(O ∨ S) ⊃ C
    2. (O ∨ S) ⊃ (A • B)
    3. ~C   / A • B

18) 1. O ⊃ (~P ∨ G)
    2. ~J ⊃ O
    3. ~(~P ∨ G) / J

19) 1. (~Z ≡ B) ⊃ ~(A ⊃ Z)
    2. ~E ⊃ (~Z ≡ B)
    3. D ⊃ (A ⊃ Z)
    4. ~E   / ~D

20) 1. ~Y ⊃ [U ⊃ (X ⊃ Y)]
    2. (~W • D) ⊃ ~Y
    3. ~U ⊃ Y
    4. ~W • D   / ~X

21) 1. (A ∨ D) ⊃ (C ∨ G)
    2. ~(~K ⊃ J) ⊃ J
    3. K ⊃ (A ∨ D)
    4. ~J   / C ∨ G

22) 1. ~(C • E) ⊃ (U • ~S)
    2. L ⊃ ~(U • ~S)
    3. ~L ⊃ [(S ∨ R) ⊃ L]
    4. ~(C • E) / ~(S ∨ R)

Exercise 9-C Proofs Using MP, MT, DS, HS

Apply the first four implication rules (MP, MT, DS, and HS) to solve these proofs. Justify all lines of the proof.

23) 1. S ∨ G
    2. ~S   / G

24) 1. ~C ⊃ ~D
    2. A ⊃ ~C   / A ⊃ ~D

25) 1. ~L ∨ ~E
    2. L
    3. E ∨ ~J   / ~J

26) 1. P ∨ ~L
    2. L ∨ D
    3. ~P   / D

27) 1. O ∨ (~H • P)
    2. ~O   / ~H • P

28) 1. B ∨ (B ∨ ~E)
    2. ~B   / ~E

29) 1. (U • K) ∨ ~N
    2. G ⊃ N
    3. ~(U • K)   / ~G

30) 1. ~L
    2. L ∨ (W ⊃ O)
    3. O ⊃ ~M   / W ⊃ ~M

31) 1. (A ∨ S) ⊃ X
    2. (~B ∨ R) ⊃ ~X
    3. ~B ∨ R   / ~(A ∨ S)

32) 1. C ⊃ ~N
    2. J ∨ (~N ⊃ L)
    3. ~J   / C ⊃ L

33) 1. T ⊃ ~W
    2. ~O ⊃ T
    3. ~H ⊃ ~O   / ~H ⊃ ~W

34) 1. (F ⊃ ~D) ⊃ (X ⊃ F)
    2. F ⊃ Y
    3. F ⊃ ~D   / X ⊃ Y

35) 1. P ∨ (Q ⊃ P)
    2. ~K ⊃ ~L
    3. (J ⊃ ~L) ⊃ ~P
    4. J ⊃ ~K   / ~Q

36) 1. W ∨ ~T
    2. ~N ⊃ T
    3. ~H
    4. H ∨ (~H ⊃ ~W)   / N

37) 1. (~E ⊃ O) ⊃ (P ⊃ M)
    2. J ∨ (~J ⊃ O)
    3. ~E ⊃ ~J
    4. ~E   / P ⊃ M

38) 1. (K • L) ∨ (~A ∨ ~C)
    2. ~(K • L)
    3. ~A ∨ (C ∨ ~T)
    4. A   / ~T

39) 1. ~(D ≡ M) ∨ ~K
    2. ~U ⊃ (D ≡ M)
    3. U ⊃ (~N ∨ G)
    4. ~(~N ∨ G)   / ~K

40) 1. ~L ∨ [X ∨ (C ⊃ X)]
    2. X ∨ (~L ⊃ ~P)
    3. X ⊃ ~P
    4. P   / C ⊃ ~P

Exercise 9-D Proofs Using 8 Rules of Implication

Apply the first **eight** implication rules (MP, MT, DS, HS, CD, Conj, Simp, Add) to solve these proofs. Justify and number all the lines of your proof.

41) 1. W • ~P
    2. ~R • ~O   / W • ~O

42) 1. ~I • M
    2. ~I ⊃ C   / C • M

43) 1. (L • R) ⊃ J
    2. L
    3. L ⊃ R   / J

44) 1. ~C • (X • ~D)
    2. A ⊃ C   / X • ~A

45) 1. K ∨ (~E • P)
    2. ~K   / ~E

46) 1. A
    2. (A ∨ S) ⊃ N   / N

47) 1. (~U • ~G) ⊃ R
    2. G ⊃ U
    3. ~U • K   / R ∨ Z

48) 1. ~L ⊃ X
    2. (L ∨ ~W) ⊃ O
    3. ~X   / O ∨ ~S

49) 1. (~B ∨ S) ⊃ R
    2. (~B • R) ⊃ ~X
    3. ~B   / ~X • R

50) 1. (I ⊃ ~D) • (X ⊃ F)
    2. I ∨ X   / ~D ∨ F

51) 1. T ⊃ ~H
    2. ~O ⊃ M
    3. T ∨ ~O   / ~H ∨ M

52) 1. (B ⊃ D) • (C ⊃ L)
    2. B   / D ∨ L

53) 1. N • (C ⊃ L)
    2. (G ⊃ S) • (~P ⊃ W)
    3. N ⊃ (G ∨ ~P)   / S ∨ W

54) 1. (~M ∨ ~T) ⊃ H
    2. P ∨ (~P ⊃ ~M)
    3. ~P   / H

55) 1. (B ∨ O) ⊃ (B ⊃ M)
    2. ~J ⊃ B
    3. E ∨ ~J
    4. ~E   / ~J ⊃ M

56) 1. (~P • Q) ⊃ (K ∨ ~C)
    2. (~P • Q) • M
    3. ~K   / ~C ∨ A

57) 1. (R ≡ A) ⊃ ~K
    2. ~U ⊃ (R ≡ A)
    3. S • (~N ∨ G)
       / S • (~U ⊃ ~K)

58) 1. ~B ∨ (~C ⊃ X)
    2. (B ∨ Z) ⊃ (L ⊃ ~B)
    3. ~C ∨ L
    4. B   / X ∨ ~S

Exercise 9-E Logic Puzzles

Translate the following arguments. Using just your common sense, try to answer the italicized question. Then apply the rules of inference to construct proofs and answer the questions.

1. If the pirate found the map, then the pirate ship sailed to Jamaica. If the pirate ship sailed to Jamaica, then the governor's daughter was kidnapped. The governor's daughter was not kidnapped. *Did the pirate find the map?*
2. If the captain found the map, then the sailor sailed to Jamaica. If the sailor sailed to Jamaica, then the sailor married the governor's daughter. The captain found the map. *Did the sailor marry the governor's daughter?*
3. Either the butler or the housekeeper murdered the guest. If the butler murdered the guest, then the driver saw the murder. If the housekeeper murdered the guest, then the maid saw the murder. If the maid saw the murder, then the maid did not tell the truth. The maid told the truth. *Who killed the guest?*
4. If the nanny went home, then the butler and the housekeeper stayed at the mansion. It is not the case that both the butler and the housekeeper stayed at the mansion. Either the nanny or the maid went home. If the maid went home, then the gardener went

home. *Who definitely went home: the nanny, the maid or the gardener (could be none of them or more than one)?*

5. Sandy must decide on seating arrangements for her wedding party: If Uncle Gene sits at the head table, then one of his brothers, either Uncle Pat or Uncle Rick, must sit at the same table. If Uncle Gene sits at the head table, then his current wife Aunt Barbara should sit at the head table, but not his former wife Aunt Alice. Uncle Gene does sit at the head table, although Uncle Rick does not. *Question: Who sits at the head table?*

6. Furthermore, either Aunt Trudy will not sit at the head table or Cousin David will not sit at the head table. If Grandma Betty does not sit at the head table, then Aunt Trudy will sit at the head table. Grandma Betty does not sit at the head table. *Question: Who sits at the head table?*

7. If Stepfather Joe does not sit at the head table, then Cousin Lou will sit at the head table. Both Cousin Beth and Cousin Lou will not sit at the head table. If the bride's mom, Mary, sits at the head table, then Grandpa Gerry will not sit at the head table. Mary must sit at the head table. *Question: Who sits at the head table?*

8. In buying a new house, Suzy must consider her budget and prioritize the amenities she most values in a home. Either she does not have granite countertops, or she does not have wooden floors. She chooses neither a pool nor an exercise room. If she does not have a pool, then she will have granite countertops. If she has an exercise room, then she must also have a dry sauna. *So, which of the following amenities does Suzy definitely choose? Circle the ones she definitely opts for. Cross out the ones she definitely decides against. If undetermined, leave alone:*

    wooden floors,   exercise room,   granite countertops,   dry sauna,   pool

9. Suzy also knows that if she does not have a library, then she can have a wine cellar. If she has a wine cellar, then she will need a casita. Suzy decides not to have a casita. If Suzy does not have a casita or does not have a rose garden, then she will have a gazebo. If she has a rose garden, then she will not have a casita. *So which does Suzy definitely choose? Circle the ones she definitely opts for. Cross out the ones she definitely decides against. If undetermined, leave alone:*

    library,   wine cellar,   casita,   rose garden,   gazebo

10. Joe must decide which woman to marry. Joe will either marry Martha or Barbie. If Joe marries Martha, then he can be assured of home-cooked meals; however, if he marries Barbie, then he can enjoy stimulating conversations. It turns out that poor Joe does not end up with stimulating conversations. *Question: What does Joe end up with?*

II. Natural Deduction: Rules of Replacement (Group II Rules) Truth-Functional Equivalences

These rules work somewhat differently from the argument patterns that make up Group I rules. Truth-functional equivalence means that two claims have the same truth-values regardless of the truth-values of their component parts. We can therefore replace them with one another while preserving the truth-values. Unlike Group I rules, which are rules of implication, rules of replacement work equally well in both directions. Also, unlike implication rules, which can only be applied to complete lines of a deduction, these rules of replacement allow us to replace any part of a line (part of a formula) with its equivalent. The metalogical symbol :: means "**is equivalent to.**"

DeMorgan's Laws (DM; rule 9) govern the negations of conjunctions and disjunctions:

~(**X** • **Y**) :: ~**X** ∨ ~**Y**
~(**X** ∨ **Y**) :: ~**X** • ~**Y**

Examples:

~(~A • B) :: A ∨ ~B
~(C ∨ ~D) :: ~C • D

Always remember to change the • to a ∨, or vice versa, when moving the ~ inside the parentheses. In the previous examples, we have omitted the double negation rule.

Commutativity (Com; rule 10) applies to conjunctions and disjunctions. The order of their elements does not matter. You may omit this rule for convenience.

X • **Y** :: **Y** • **X**
X ∨ **Y** :: **Y** ∨ **X**

Examples:
~A • B :: B • ~A
C ∨ (D ∨ ~E) :: C ∨ (~E ∨ D)

Associativity (Assoc; rule 11) tells us that strings of conjuncts or disjuncts may be grouped differently by moving the parentheses:

X • (**Y** • **Z**) :: (**X** • **Y**) • **Z**
X ∨ (**Y** ∨ **Z**) :: (**X** ∨ **Y**) ∨ **Z**

Example
(A ∨ B) ∨ ~C :: A ∨ (B ∨ ~C)

The two versions of **distribution** (Dist; rule 12) let us handle combinations of conjunction and disjunction, as follows:

X • (Y ∨ Z) :: (X • Y) ∨ (Y • Z)
X ∨ (Y • Z) :: (X ∨ Y) • (X ∨ Z)

Examples
A • (∼B ∨ C) :: (A • ∼B) ∨ (A • ∼C)
∼D ∨ (∼E • F) :: (∼D ∨ ∼E) • (∼D ∨ F)

Double negation (DN; rule 13) allows you to remove two consecutive tildes or insert two tildes into a formula. You may omit this rule for convenience.

X :: ∼∼X

Example
∼A • B :: ∼∼A • ∼∼B

There are five more rules of replacement that we will not cover: transposition, material implication, material equivalence, exportation, and tautology. Thus, our proof theory will be incomplete as part of the natural deduction system will not be included in this chapter.

Exercise 9-F Apply Rules of Replacement

With the rules of replacement, you may substitute a whole line or part of a line with an equivalent formula.

9. **De Morgan's Rule (DM)**

   (X • Y) is equivalent to ∼X ∨ ∼Y
   ∼**(X ∨ Y)** is equivalent to ∼X • ∼Y

   ∼(____ • ____)   ____ ∨ ____
   ∼(____ ∨ ____)   ____ • ____

   ∼(A • ∼R)   ∼(∼B ∨ J)   ∼S ∨ ∼G   ∼Z • M

   (B ∨ D) ≡ ∼S   (∼A • R) ⊃ ∼(B ∨ C)

10. Commutativity (Com)

You may omit this rule.

X • Y is equivalent to **Y • X**
X ∨ Y is equivalent to **Y ∨ X**

| A • ~B | ~C ∨ ~D | ~(~E ∨ F) | (~G ⊃ H) • ~(I • J) |

11. Associativity (Assoc)

X • (Y • Z) is equivalent to **(X • Y) • Z**
X ∨ (Y ∨ Z) is equivalent to **(X ∨ Y) ∨ Z**

| ~A • (B • ~C) | D ∨ (~E ∨ ~F) | (I ≡ ~G) • (H • I) |

12. Distribution (Dist)

X • (Y ∨ Z) is equivalent to **(X • Y) ∨ (X • Z)**
X ∨ (Y • Z) is equivalent to **(X ∨ Y) • (X ∨ Z)**

| S ∨ (I • ~J) | (B ∨ D) • (B ∨ ~S) | ~R • (~N ∨ ~K) |

13. Double Negation (DN)

X is equivalent to **~~X**
You may omit this rule.

| ~~J | R | N ∨ ~~K |

Here are some proof solutions, which include the replacement rules, followed by some guidelines.

1. (A ∨ D) ⊃ L
2. ~L   / ~D
3. ~(A ∨ D)   1, 2, MT
4. ~A • ~D   3, DM
5. ~D   4, Simp

In line 1, the main operator is a horseshoe, and the formula in line 2 is the negation of the consequent of line 1. This allows us to apply MT and to derive the negation of the antecedent A ∨ D. The negation of a disjunction having the form ~(X ∨ Y) should remind us of DM. Lastly, since the main operator of line 4 is a dot, we may derive either of the conjuncts.

1. (K ∨ S) • (K ∨ E)
2. ~(S • E)   / K ∨ ~L

3. K ∨ (S • E)   1, Dist
4. K   2, 3, DS
5. K ∨ ~L   4, Add

In line 1, we apply Dist since we notice the common element K ∨ that appears in both sets of parentheses. Although we may be tempted to apply DM to line 2, it won't help us to solve the proof. However, line 2 is the negation of one of the disjuncts in line 3, allowing us to apply DS. Another clue that line 3 may call for a DS is that the main operator of line 3 is a wedge ∨.

1. (D ∨ K) ⊃ ~R
2. ~R ⊃ ~(Z • ~G)
3. D ∨ (M • K)   / ~Z ∨ G
4. (D ∨ M) • (D ∨ K)   3, Dist
5. D ∨ K   4, Simp
6. ~R   1, 5, MP
7. ~(Z • ~G)   2, 6, MP
8. ~Z ∨ G   7, DM

Memorizing the rules will help us recognize when certain rules are applicable. If you remove all the capital letters and negated letters, we see the form of line 3 as ∨ (•). This main structure of the formula should remind us of Dist. Having applied Dist to line 3, we end up in line 4 with a formula having a dot as the main operator such that we can readily derive the formula from either side of the main operator dot. It is the second conjunct D ∨ K that we wish to obtain because it is the antecedent of line 1. Then applying MP to lines 1 and 5 gives us the consequent ~R. Another application of MP to lines 2 and 6 gives us the longer consequent ~(Z • ~G). This time the skeleton ~(•) in line 7 should remind us of DM, which when applied results in the desired conclusion.

There are also interesting structures in this next proof with the skeleton (•) ∨ (•) relating to Dist, while • (•) is a structure relating to Assoc.

1. (Q ≡ S) ⊃ [(~E • B) ∨ (~E • ~H)]
2. ~(Q ≡ S) ⊃ ~N
3. ~C • (~J • N)   / ~E
4. (~C • ~J) • N   3, Assoc
5. N   4, Simp
6. Q ≡ S   2, 5, MT
7. (~E • B) ∨ (~E • ~H)   1, 6, MP
8. ~E • (B ∨ ~H)   7, Dist
9. ~E   8, Simp

In lines 1 and 2, there are horseshoes as the main operator. The rules that involve horseshoes include MP, MT, and HS. However, since there is no diagonal match with lines 1 and 2, HS is not applicable. What we then need is either the antecedent of lines 1 or 2 to allow for MP or the negation of their consequents for MT. We can derive N from line 3 by first applying Assoc, followed by Simp. Two applications of Simp could also be the way to obtain N from line 3. After deriving N, MT using lines 2 and 5 is our next step. We then have Q ≡ S in line 6, and since it is the antecedent of line 1, we can apply MP to obtain line 7. We end the proof with Dist and Simp.

Sometimes it helps to work backward and free the conclusion letters as they appear in the premises. The conclusion of the next proof is R • J. Let's work on isolating the letters R and J from the premises and then joining them by the Conj rule.

1. ~(S ∨ ~M)
2. (R ∨ ~M) • (L ∨ ~C)
3. (M ∨ H) ⊃ J   / R • J
4. ~S • M   1, DM
5. M   4, Simp
6. R ∨ ~M   2, Simp
7. R   5, 6, DS
8. M ∨ H   5, Add
9. J   3, 8, MP
10. R • J   7, 9, Conj

It is important to distinguish implication rules (MP, MT, DS, HS, CD, Simp, Conj, Add) from replacement rules (DM, Dist, Assoc, Com, DN). While implication rules apply to whole formulas and their main operators, replacement rules allow us to substitute subformulas with equivalent formulas. With rules of replacement, subformulas within the parentheses, as well as whole formulas, may be replaced. For example, consider the formula (A • B) • C. We could apply the replacement rule of Com to the subformula (A • B), converting it to (B • A). Then just a part of the formula would be replaced but the rest of it would remain the same, resulting in the new equivalent formula (B • A) • C. We also could apply the replacement rule of Assoc to the whole formula (A • B) • C and obtain the equivalent formula A • (B • C). We will solve the following proofs in such a way that we highlight the difference between implication and replacement rules.

1. (B ∨ ~M) ⊃ S
2. L ∨ (~G ⊃ L)
3. H ⊃ ~(~B • M)
4. (H ⊃ S) ⊃ ~L   / G
5. H ⊃ (B ∨ ~M)   3, DM
6. H ⊃ S   1, 5, HS
7. ~L   4, 6, MP
8. ~G ⊃ L   2, 7, DS
9. G   2, 8, MT

In the next proof, the strategy of working backward can be helpful when it is unclear where to start.

1. (P ∨ ~M) ⊃ ~S
2. (J • ~D) ∨ S
3. [(N ⊃ ~Z) • P] • ~(J • T)   / ~(D ∨ ~P)

The conclusion is ~(D ∨ ~P), and it has a structure that should remind us of DM. By DM, we know that the conclusion is equivalent to ~D • P. To form a conjunction where the dot is the main operator, it would suffice to prove ~D on its own line and P on a different line. Thus, our intermediate goal is to derive ~D and P on separate lines. We find ~D in line 2 and P in line 3. We cannot free ~D from line 2 by Simp because the wedge ∨ is the main operator. However, we can isolate P from line 3 by two applications of Simp. Then with Add, we can obtain the antecedent of line 1. Once we derive ~S, the problem of freeing ~D from line 2 may become more apparent. The solution to the proof may look like this:

1. (P ∨ ~M) ⊃ ~S
2. (J • ~D) ∨ S
3. [(N ⊃ ~Z) • P] • ~(J • T)   / ~(D ∨ ~P)
4. (N ⊃ ~Z) • P   3, Simp
5. P   4, Simp
6. P ∨ ~M   5, Add
7. ~S   1, 6, MP
8. J • ~D   2, 7, DS
9. ~D   2, Simp
10. ~D • P   5, 9, Conj
11. ~(D ∨ ~P)   10, DM

Solving proofs is a skill that may be developed by becoming familiar with the rules and by continual practice. It is best to begin with easier problems and work your way to more complex proofs. In time, the patterns of valid inferences will be easier to find, and you will have developed the art of strategic thinking.

Exercise 9-G Proofs Using 18 Rules of Inference

Apply 18 rules of inference to solve these proofs. Justify and number all the lines of your proof. You may omit DN and Com. A hint is provided for each proof.

59) DM
1. (E ∨ P) ⊃ R
2. ~(~E • ~P)   / R

60) DM
1. ~I ⊃ (~L • T)
2. ~(L ∨ ~T) ⊃ M
   / ~I ⊃ M

61) DM
1. (~B ∨ S) ⊃ R
2. L • ~R   / ~S

62) DM
1. ~(~I • J)
2. (I ∨ ~J) ⊃ ~C
   / ~C ∨ T

63) DM
1. K ∨ ~(E ∨ ~P)
2. ~K   / ~E ∨ ~Y

64) DM
1. (~A ∨ ~S) ⊃ ~X
2. ~(~H ∨ G)
3. ~(A • S)   / ~(X ∨ G)

65) Dist
1. P ∨ (L • Y)
2. (P ∨ L) ⊃ I   / I

66) Dist
1. (E ⊃ J) • (U ⊃ C)
2. E ∨ (U • A)   / J ∨ C

67) Dist
1. (C ∨ D) • (C ∨ L)
2. [C ∨ (D • L)] ⊃ ~N
3. E ∨ (N • A)   / ~N • E

68) Dist
1. (H • B) ∨ (H • C)
2. ~H ∨ ~R   / ~R

69) Dist
1. ~E ⊃ I
2. (~I • P) ∨ (~I • G)
3. T ∨ ~E   / ~(~T ∨ I)

70) Dist
1. [D • (C ∨ J)] ⊃ S
2. (D • C) ∨ (D • J)
3. S ⊃ R   / R • (C ∨ J)

71) Assoc
1. (D ∨ G) ∨ ~L
2. ~D   / ~(~G • L)

72) Assoc
1. (S • B) ∨ D
2. ~S ∨ (~B ∨ N)
3. ~R • ~N   / D ∨ M

73) Assoc
1. [R • (~A • J)] ⊃ H
2. (R • ~A) • J
3. (H ∨ ~B) ⊃ C   / C • H

CHAPTER 10
Truth Tables (Indirect or Short Method)

The regular truth table method can become quite lengthy as more simple statements or capital letters are involved. Since the number of rows required in the truth table increases exponentially with the number of capital letters, truth tables for very complex formulas may become too cumbersome. Fortunately, there is an alternative method called the indirect truth table method (also called the short or abbreviated truth table) that can provide us with a shortcut.

With the indirect truth table method, we must apply the same truth value definitions of the five logical operators. Recall the truth-functional definitions of logical operators:

~	opposite truth value	1 way True	1 way False
•	True only when **T • T**	**1 way True**	3 ways False
∨	False only when **F ∨ F**	3 ways True	**1 way False**
⊃	False only when **T ⊃ F**	3 ways True	**1 way False**
≡	True when T ≡ T and F ≡ F	2 ways True	2 ways False

Our goal with indirect truth tables will be similar to our objective for regular truth tables. We are still interested in finding whether it is possible for a given argument to have true premises and a false conclusion. If it is possible, then there would exist at least one row in our regular truth table in which all the premises are true (under the main operator), while the conclusion is false (under the main operator). Such a row we had called "the invalidating row." This row of only true premises and a false conclusion is also referred to as a counterexample of the argument. There can be one or more of these rows or counterexamples in an invalid argument. The existence of at least one such row means that the argument is invalid.

With the indirect truth table method, we will try to create this invalidating row without having to construct the whole truth table. One invalidating row suffices to show that an argument is invalid; once we have identified one invalidating row, there would then be no need to examine the other rows in the table. Thus, the indirect truth table is a shortcut that saves us needless time and effort.

The indirect truth table method applies steps similar to the regular truth table method but in reverse. That is, we work backward to create the invalidating row. We begin by assuming that the argument is invalid and that there is an invalidating row. The first step is to write "True" under the main operator of each premise and "False" under the main operator of the conclusion. Consider an argument with two premises:

Example One

A ⊃ B /   A ∨ ∼B //   B ⊃ C
  T   **T**   **F**

Next, we work backward to determine the separate truth-values of each capital letter. Although there may be more than one way to proceed, it is generally best to target the formulas with the least number of possibilities. In this example, there are three ways to make the first premise true given the definition of ⊃ and there are also three ways to make the second premise true given the definition of ∨. However, there is only one way to make the conclusion false because ⊃ is false only when we have T ⊃ F combination.

A ⊃ B /   A ∨ ∼B //   B ⊃ C
  T   T   **T** F **F**

Once the truth-values of some capital letters have been determined, we should locate where else those same capital letters appear in the formulas and enter the same truth-values under those capital letters.

A ⊃ B /   A ∨ ∼B //   B ⊃ C
T **T**   T **T**   **T** F F

Now, there are two possibilities for the first premise to be true given that B is true. In the first premise, A could either be true or false. In the second premise, we face fewer possibilities. Since B is true, ∼B must be false.

A ⊃ B /   A ∨ ∼B //   B ⊃ C
T T   T **F** T   T F F

Having determined ∼B is false, there is only one possibility for making the ∨ true. In the second premise, A must be true. If A is true in the second premise, then A must also be true in the first premise.

A ⊃ B /   A ∨ ∼B //   B ⊃ C
T T T   **T** T F T   T F F

In the end, we must double-check that we have indeed constructed an invalidating row. We should check that there are no problems or contradictions in any of the formulas. Do all the letters have the same truth-values? Do any of the truth-values contradict the truth-functional definitions of any of the logical operators? If there are no problems with the row we constructed, then we can conclude that there is an invalidating row that exists for the argument and, therefore, the argument is invalid. If we were forced into a contradiction, and there is no possible way to create an invalidating row, then we have shown that the argument must be valid.

Next, let us consider what would happen if the argument in question is a valid one. Obviously, we would not be able to construct an invalidating row for a valid argument, for no such row would exist. The following example is a valid argument, and we begin as before by making the premise main operators true and the conclusion main operator false.

Example Two

~A ⊃ ~B   /   ~A   //   ~B
   T   **T**   **F**

Next, there is some choice as to where to go. At this point, the easiest formulas to determine are the second premise and the conclusion. It does not matter which we choose to do first.

~A ⊃ ~B   /   ~A   //   ~B
  T   T **F**   F **T**

After having determined the truth-values of A and B, we need to enter the same truth-values wherever the same capital letters appear:

~A ⊃ ~B   /   ~A   //   ~B
F T T   T F   F T

We can then finish off the first premise, as shown below, by applying the definition of ~. If A is false, ~A is true and, if B is true, then ~B is false.

~A ⊃ ~B   /   ~A   //   ~B
<u>T **F** T **F**</u> T   T F   F T

We see from our resulting attempt to build an invalidating row that there is a problem with the first premise. When we double-check for contradictions, we should notice that the antecedent of the first premise is true, while the consequent is false. This would make the main operator (⊃) of the first premise false, not true! In trying to build an invalidating row, we were forced into a contradiction, which is underlined. Thus, if the attempt to make the premises true and the conclusion false necessarily leads to a contradiction, it is not possible for the premises to be true and the conclusion false, in which case the argument must be valid. As a result, we have proven the validity of the previous argument without having to build all four rows of the regular truth table method.

It seems a little confusing that when we run into a contradiction (a bad thing), we conclude that the argument is valid (good). Similarly, when we do not run into a contradiction (a good thing), we conclude that the argument is invalid (bad). However, we should keep in mind that our original intent was to build an invalidating row, which is "a bad thing" as far as arguments go. Successfully creating this "bad thing" (the invalidating row) means the argument is indeed "bad" or invalid. If we run into problems attempting to create this "bad thing" (the invalidating row), then that means the argument is "good" or valid.

I. Steps for the Indirect Truth Table Method

1. Try to build the invalidating row. Under the premise main operators, write T; under the conclusion main operator, write F.
2. Go to the easiest formulas first (ones with the least number of possibilities).
3. Enter the value of the capital letters once they have been determined.
4. At the end, check for problems or contradictions with the invalidating row.
   a. No contradiction means there is an invalidating row, and the argument is invalid.
   b. Contradiction means there's no invalidating row, and the argument is valid.

Exercise 10-A Indirect Truth Tables (One Row)

These problems are examples of "one-line" indirect truth tables. Later we will work on indirect truth tables that call for more than one line.

1. B ⊃ A   /   ~A   //   ~B ≡ C

2. (A ⊃ B) • (C ⊃ D)   /   A ∨ C   //   B ∨ D

3. ~A ⊃ (B ∨ C)   /   ~B   //   C ⊃ A

4. ~(A ⊃ B)   /   B ⊃ A   /   A ⊃ ~B   //   A • ~B

5. A ∨ B   /   C ⊃ ~D   /   A ∨ C   //   ~(~B • D)

Some indirect truth tables are more complex than the preceding ones because more than one line may be required to prove validity or invalidity. In our next example, Example Three, we reach a point when there is no longer a "one possibility" option.

Example Three

~ (A ≡ B) // ~ (A ⊃ B)
T   **F**

As before, write true under premise main operators and false under conclusion main operator.

~ (A ≡ B) // ~ (A ⊃ B)
T **F**   F **T**

Within the parentheses, we can determine the values of the inner logical operators.

But now, which is the easier formula to work with? Which one has fewer possibilities? So, we must consider how many ways to make (A ≡ B) false versus how many ways to make (A ⊃ B) true. There are two ways to make (A ≡ B) false, but three ways to make (A ⊃ B) true. We should then focus on making (A ≡ B) false because considering two ways is easier than three ways.

~ (A ≡ B) // ~ (A ⊃ B)
T   F   F   T
T   F   F   T

Proceed by writing what we have so far on the next line so that we have the same row repeated twice.

~ (A ≡ B) // ~ (A ⊃ B)
T **T F F**   F   T
T **F F T**   F   T

Now in Row 1, we write one way to make (A ≡ B) false, and in Row 2, we write the other way.

~(A ≡ B) // ~(A ⊃ B)
T T F F   F <u>**T T F**</u>
T F F T   F   T

Let's try to create an invalidating row in Row 1. If we succeed, then we have one invalidating row, and there will be no need to continue with Row 2.

However, Row 1 does not provide us with an invalidating row because we are forced into a contradiction in the conclusion. The problem is that, if A is true and B is false, then the conditional statement (A ⊃ B) is not true. We must continue to the second line and check whether Row 2 is an invalidating row. We cannot say the argument is valid until we have exhausted all the possibilities and find that it is impossible to create the invalidating row.

~ (A ≡ B) // ~ (A ⊃ B)
T T F F   F <u>T T F</u>
T F F T   F **F T T**

Continue with Row 2. After checking for problems in Row 2, we find that it is an invalidating row, so the argument is invalid!

118 | Basics of Logic

Example Four
This is an argument that is valid but will require three rows. We begin with writing True under the main operator of each premise and False under the main operator of the conclusion. In the second premise, we have also determined that the dot is False since the tilde outside the parentheses is True.

```
B ∨ A  /  ~(A • ~B)  /  B ⊃ C  //  C • B
   T        T   F            T          F
```

This time, the least number of possibilities involves three ways. There's no easier option. Let's start with a formula that looks relatively short. We might pick the first, third, or fourth formula. If we consider the first premise, we can write out the three ways to make (B ∨ A) true. Let us copy what we have so far two more times so that we have a total of three rows.

```
B ∨ A  /  ~(A • ~B)  /  B ⊃ C  //  C • B
   T        T   F            T          F
   T        T   F            T          F
   T        T   F            T          F
```

Now we may write out the three ways to make the first premise true. The main operator in the first premise is a wedge ∨, and it is false only when there is at least one true disjunct (T ∨ T, T ∨ F, or F ∨ T).

```
B ∨ A  /  ~(A • ~B)  /  B ⊃ C  //  C • B
T T T       T   F            T          F
T T F       T   F            T          F
F T T       T   F            T          F
```

Then continue to work the problem one row at a time. We can stop once we find the invalidating row. In this case, we need to solve for all three rows to prove that the argument is valid.

```
B ∨ A  /  ~(A • ~B)  /  B ⊃ C  //  C • B
T T T     T T F F T     T T T     T F T      ⇐ Problem in conclusion
T T F     T F F F T     T T F     F F T      ⇐ Problem in third premise
F T T     T T F T F     F T       F F        ⇐ Problem in second premise
```

We tried all three possibilities and found that it is impossible to build an invalidating row for this argument. In each row, we were forced into a contradiction, indicated by the underlined truth-values. Therefore, we conclude that this argument is valid. There are different paths or sequences we can take to prove this argument is valid. No matter how we solve this problem, we will run into a contradiction in each of the three rows. The contradiction that we run into may involve different formulas than the ones we see in the solution above. If we proceed in a different order and consider the three ways to make the dot in the conclusion False, our solution may look like this:

```
B ∨ A   /   ∼(A • ∼B)   /   B ⊃ C   //   C • B
F T T      T T F T F         F T T         T F F        ⇐ Problem in second premise
T T        T   F F T         T T F         F F T        ⇐ Problem in third premise
F T F      T F F T F         F T F         F F F        ⇐ Problem in first premise
```

Try the problem again using a different sequence:

B ∨ A   /   ∼(A • ∼B)   /   B ⊃ C   //   C • B

_____

_____

B ∨ A   /   ∼(A • ∼B)   /   B ⊃ C   //   C • B

_____

_____

In the next problem, we will find that an invalidating row is possible for we can successfully make all the premises true while the conclusion is false.

```
∼A ∨ ∼(A • B)  /  (∼B ≡ C) ⊃ D  //  ∼D ∨ B
       T                   T              F
```

After we make each premise main operator True and the conclusion main operator False, we find that the easiest formula with the least number of possibilities is the conclusion. There is only one way to make a wedge False: F ∨ F. We write 'F' under the ∼ and 'F' under the B.

```
∼A ∨ ∼(A • B)  /  (∼B ≡ C) ⊃ ∼D  //  ∼D ∨ B
       T                   T           F  F F
```

Consequently, since ∼D is False in the conclusion, D must be True. We then write 'T' under the D's. Furthermore, since B is False in the conclusion, B must be false wherever else it appears in the argument. So, we write 'F' under each occurrence of B.

∼A ∨ ∼(A • ∼B) / (∼A ≡ C) ⊃ ∼D // ∼D ∨ B
 T   F   T   T   F**T**F F

Thus, ∼B must be True since B is False. On the other hand, ∼D must be False since D is true.

∼A ∨ ∼(A • ∼B) / (∼A ≡ C) ⊃ ∼D // ∼D ∨ B
 T   T F   T **F**T   F T F F

Given that the conditional in the second premise must be true and its consequent is False, the antecedent must be True. For if the antecedent were True while the consequent is False, the second premise would not be True. Accordingly, we write 'F' under the main operator of the antecedent, which is the triple bar ≡.

∼A ∨ ∼(A • ∼B) / (∼A ≡ C) ⊃ ∼D // ∼D ∨ B
 T   T F   **F**   T F T   F T F F

At this point, we find that there are three ways to make the wedge ∨ of the first premise True, and there are two ways to make the triple bar ≡ of the second premise False. Since two is fewer rows than three, we focus on how to make the triple bar ≡ False.

∼A ∨ ∼(A • ∼B) / (∼A ≡ C) ⊃ ∼D // ∼D ∨ B
 T   T F   **F**   T F T   F T F F

Since we must consider two ways to make the triple bar False, we need to copy the row we have so far one more time so that we have two of the same row under the argument.

∼A ∨ ∼(A • ∼B) / (∼A ≡ C) ⊃ ∼D // ∼D ∨ B
 T   T F   F   T F T   F T F F
 T   T F   F   T F T   F T F F

One way to make the triple bar False is T ∨ F and the other is F ∨ T. Thus, we enter values under ∼A and C.

∼A ∨ ∼(A • ∼B) / (∼A ≡ C) ⊃ ∼D // ∼D ∨ B
 T   T F   **T** F **F** T F T   F T F F
 T   T F   **F** F **T** T F T   F T F F

Finally, we determine that A is False in the first row and True in the second row. Then we may complete our indirect truth table. Although the second row contains a contradiction, the first row shows the argument is invalid.

∼A ∨ ∼(A • ∼B) / (∼A ≡ C) ⊃ ∼D // ∼D ∨ B
T F T T F F T F   **T** F F **F** T F T   F T F F
F T T T <u>T F T F</u>   **F** T F **T** T F T   F T F F

Exercise 10-B Indirect Truth Tables (Multiple Rows)

Please apply the indirect truth table method to determine the validity or invalidity of the argument. The indirect truth table may consist of one to three rows. Note that the number of lines does not indicate how many rows we will actually need.

1. ~(A ≡ B) • ~C   //   ~(B ∨ ~A)

2. R ⊃ E   /   (D ≡ E) • ~S   //   D ∨ ~R

3. ~(J ≡ K)   /   ~N • ~(E ⊃ L)   /   ~K ∨ ~L   //   J • ~K

4. (A ∨ B) • (B ⊃ A)   /   ~A ∨ ~B   //   ~(A ⊃ B)

5. (~K ≡ J) • A   /   B ∨ ~J   //   (~B ⊃ ~K) ∨ ~L

6. ~B ⊃ A / ~A ∨ B / (B ⊃ C) • D // (C • B) ∨ ~D

7. (Q • ~X) • (S ⊃ J) / ~(~S ∨ R) / ~R ≡ W // W ⊃ ~J

8. ~(A ∨ B) / ~(B ≡ ~D) • ~E / ~E ≡ ~B // ~(A ⊃ C)

9. S ⊃ (H • E) / G ∨ ~A / ~(G ≡ H) // ~S

10. (K ⊃ ~J) • (K ∨ J) / J ⊃ K / ~L ∨ M // L ⊃ (J • K)

Bibliography

Bergmann, Merrie, James Moor, and Jack Nelson. *The Logic Book.* 6th ed. New York: McGraw-Hill Companies, 2013.

Curry, Haskell B. *Foundations of Mathematical Logic.* New York: Dover Publications, Inc., 1977.

Halbach, Volker. *The Logic Manual.* New York: Oxford University Press, 2015.

Howard-Snyder, Frances, Daniel Howard-Snyder, and Ryan Wasserman. *The Power of Logic.* 5th ed. New York: McGraw-Hill Companies, 2013.

Hurley, Patrick J. *A Concise Introduction to Logic.* 2nd ed. Belmont, CA: Wadsworth Pub. Co., 1985.

Johnson, Robert M. *A Logic Book.* 3rd ed. Belmont, CA: Wadsworth Pub. Co., 1999.

Kahane, Howard, and Nancy Cavender. *Logic and Contemporary Rhetoric.* Belmont, CA: Wadsworth Pub. Co., 1998.

Kalish, Donald, and Richard Montague. *Logic: Techniques of Formal Reasoning.* New York: Harcourt, Brace & World, 1964.

Kelley, David. *The Art of Reasoning.* New York: W.W. Norton & Company, Inc., 2014.

Layman, Stephen C. *The Power of Logic.* New York: McGraw-Hill Companies, 2005.

Malpass, Alex, and Marianna Antonutti Marfori. *The History of Philosophical and Formal Logic from Aristotle to Tarski.* New York: Bloomsbury Academic Publishing, 2018.

Marcus, Russell. *Introduction to Formal Logic with Philosophical Applications.* New York: Oxford University Press, 2010.

Moore, Brooke, and Richard Parker. *Critical Thinking.* 7th ed. New York: McGraw-Hill Companies, 2001.

Morrow, David, and Anthony Weston. *A Workbook for Arguments.* 2nd ed. Indianapolis, Cambridge: Hackett Publishing Company, 2016.

Sider, Theodore. *Logic for Philosophy.* New York: Oxford University Press, 2010.

Teller, Paul. *A Modern Formal Logic Primer: Sentence Logic, Volume 1.* New Jersey: Prentice Hall, 1989.

www.ingramcontent.com/pod-product-compliance
Lightning Source LLC
Chambersburg PA
CBHW080413300426
44113CB00015B/2498